William Willis

The Law of negotiable Securities

Six lectures delivered at the Request of the Council of Legal Education

William Willis

The Law of negotiable Securities
Six lectures delivered at the Request of the Council of Legal Education

ISBN/EAN: 9783337018139

Printed in Europe, USA, Canada, Australia, Japan

Cover: Foto ©Suzi / pixelio.de

More available books at **www.hansebooks.com**

THE LAW

OF

NEGOTIABLE SECURITIES.

SIX LECTURES

DELIVERED AT THE REQUEST OF

THE COUNCIL OF LEGAL EDUCATION.

BY

WILLIAM WILLIS,

ONE OF HER MAJESTY'S COUNSEL.

LONDON:
STEVENS & HAYNES,
Law Publishers,
13, BELL YARD, TEMPLE BAR.
1896.

PREFACE.

In the year 1895, the Council of Legal Education decided to make arrangements for the delivery from time to time of lectures on some legal subject, to which not only students of the four Inns of Court should be admitted, but also practising barristers and the general public.

I was invited by the Council to deliver the first course. The invitation was communicated to me by Lord Justice Lindley, then the Chairman of the Council, who, with kind and encouraging words, asked me to accept it. I did so, and with the consent of the Council, I chose as my subject "The Law of Negotiable Securities."

In accepting the invitation, I said that I had neither the time nor the inclination to prepare written lectures, but that I would, without verbal preparation, present to my hearers the law, such as it had shaped itself in my mind as the result of reading and practice. The condition was approved. The lectures were delivered during last Michaelmas Sittings, and whatever interest they awakened was chiefly due, in my opinion, to the fact that they were spoken, and not written. The reader of these lectures should remember that in perusing them he is reading spoken discourse.

It was suggested by one or two of my friends that the lectures should be published, in order that their publication might serve as a memorial of the noble design of the Council of Legal Education to make the learning and resources of the Inns of Court available for the widest diffusion of legal knowledge.

To be a fitting memorial of the new departure, they ought to have been delivered by someone with more leisure and greater ability.

The lectures were taken down in shorthand and have received such revision as their publication rendered necessary.

In the work of revision I have frequently consulted my friend Mr. Arthur Cohen, Q.C., who readily placed at my disposal both his learning and judgment.

The proof-sheets of the lectures have been read by my friends of the Common Law Bar, Mr. Julian Robins, Mr. Joseph Hurst and Mr. George Henry Mallinson, and I have availed myself in many instances of their suggestions.

To Mr. Patrick Thomas Blackwell, Barrister-at-Law, of the Inner Temple, I am indebted for the preparation of the Index and List of Cases.

To all these gentlemen I offer my sincere thanks for their generous assistance, and commend the little volume to the favourable consideration of all those who may read it.

WILLIAM WILLIS.

May, 1896.

TABLE OF CONTENTS.

	PAGE
PREFACE . . , . .	v
TABLE OF CASES	ix

LECTURE I.

What is meant when a security or instrument is said to be negotiable 1

LECTURE II.

Principal instruments comprised under the head of negotiable securities 30

LECTURE III.

Bills of Exchange. Contractual obligations valid at Common Law which cannot be the subject of a Bill of Exchange. Transactions which can be effected by a Bill of Exchange which cannot be carried out by the rules of the Common Law or Equity. Incidents and privileges of Bills of Exchange which do not attach to contracts at Common Law 5

LECTURE IV.

Form of Bill of Exchange. Parties thereto—Drawer: drawee: acceptor: payee. Consideration for a Bill of Exchange— Bill must be drawn for an ascertained sum of money. Qualified or conditional drawing: qualified or conditional acceptance. Form of acceptance: in writing and on face of the bill: duties of holder of qualified acceptance. Days of grace: effect of acceptance on debt for which it is given: only drawee can be acceptor 97

LECTURE V.

How the property in a bill of exchange may be transferred: past debt may be consideration for transfer: bill of exchange payable on demand valid, although given for an antecedent debt. Meaning of indorsement of a bill: indorsement on blank: special endorsement: restrictive and conditional endorsements: obligations of a transferor who is not an endorser; partial endorsement—transferee of an over-due bill takes subject to the equities attaching to the bill: burden of proof cast on holder of a bill when fraud or improper dealing in connection with the bill is established—presentment of bill for acceptance 125

LECTURE VI.

Presentment for payment: rules relating thereto: when excused: notice of dishonour: necessary to charge drawer and endorsers: how notice of dishonour given and in what form: time for giving such notice: promissory notes: in what respects they differ from bills of exchange: cheques: relation of banker and customer: points in which cheques differ from bills of exchange: payment made by forged signature of the drawer and forged signature of the indorser: crossed cheques: cheques marked "not negotiable" . . 153

INDEX 187

TABLE OF CASES.

	PAGE
BAXENDALE v. Bennett, L. R. 3 Q. B. D. 525	62, 63, 112
Belshaw v. Bush, 11 C. B. 191	127
Bentinck v. London Joint Stock Bank, L. R. (1893) 2 Ch. 120	48
Bickerdike v. Bollman, 2 Sm. L. C. 10th Edit. 99	157, 158, 161
Blakely Ordnance Co., *In re*, L. R. 3 Ch. 154	98
Bobbett v. Pinkett, L. R. 1 Ex. D. 368	182
Brandao v. Barnett, 12 Cl. & F. 787	37, 38
Buller v. Crips, 6 Mod. 29. *See* ERRATUM.	
CADY v. London Chartered Bank of Australia, L. R. 38 Ch. D. 388 ; 15 App. Ca. 267	48
Carter v. Flower, 16 M. & W. 743	158
Crofts v. Beale, 11 C. B. 172	126, 127
Cronch v. Crédit Foncier, L. R. 8 Q. B. 374	34, 36, 37, 47, 50, 54
Currie v. Misa, L. R. 10 Ex. 153	127
DAVIS v. Clarke, 13 L. J. Q. B. 305 ; 6 Q. B. 16	100, 119
EASTON v. London Joint Stock Bank, L. R. 34 Ch. D. 95	5, 14, 48
Edie v. East India Co., 2 Burr. 1216	33, 34
FIELDER v. Marshall, 9 C. B. N. S. 606	119
Fuentes v. Montis, L. R. 3 C. P. 268	56
GARRARD v. Lewis, L. R. 10 Q. B. D. 30	63, 103
Glyn v. Baker, 13 Ea. 509	40
Goodwin v. Robarts, L. R. 10 Ex. 76; *Ib.* 337; 1 App. Ca. 476	14, 36, 44, 45, 46, 47
Gorgier v. Mieville, 3 B. & C. 45	36, 42, 45, 47
Grant v. Vaughan, 3 Burr. 1516	33
Gray v. Milner, 8 Taunt. 739	118
Gurney v. Behrend, 3 E. & B. 622	56
—— v. Womersley, 4 E. & B. 133	134

TABLE OF CASES.

	PAGE
HALL v. Featherstone, 3 H. & N. 284	143
Hartley v. Case, 4 B. & C. 339	164
Hayward, In re, L. R. 6 Ch. 546	110
Hogarth v. Latham, L. R. 3 Q. B. D. 643	112
Holmes v. Kidd, 3 H. & N. 891	141
Hopkins v. Logan, 5 M. & W. 241	70
INGHAM v. Primrose, 7 C. B. N. S. 82	61, 62, 63
JACKSON v. Hudson, 2 Camp. 447	64, 116
Jones v. Gordon, L. R. 2 App. Ca. 616	26
KEENE v. Beard, 8 C. B. N. S. 372	171
LITTLE v. London Joint Stock Bank, L. R. (1891) 1 Ch. 270	50
London & County Banking Co. v. London & River Plate Bank, L. R. 20 Q. B. D. 232; 21 Q. B. D. 535	7, 47
Lysaght v. Bryant, 9 C. B. 46	132
MANGLES v. Dixon, 3 H. L. Ca. 702	76, 77
Marston v. Allen, 8 M. & W. 494	131
Miller v. Race, 1 Sm. L. C. (10th Edit.) 447	57
NATAL INVESTMENT Co., In re, L. R. 3 Ch. 355	98
OGDEN v. Benas, L. R. 9 C. P. 513	176
PARTRIDGE v. Bank of England, 9 Q. B. 396	38, 39, 40
Paul v. Joel, 3 H. & N. 455; 4 H. & N. 355	164
Percival v. Dunn, L. R. 29 Ch. D. 128	72
Peto v. Reynolds, 9 Ex. 410	101
RAPHAEL v. Bank of England, 17 C. B. 161	20, 22
Reg. v. Hawkes, 2 Moo. C. C. 60	101
Royal Bank of Scotland v. Tottenham, L. R. (1894), 2 Q. B. 715	174
Rumball v. Metropolitan Bank, L. R. 2 Q. B. D. 194	10, 36, 37
SANDERSON v. Piper, 5 Bing. N. C. 425	103
Scholfield v. Londesborough (Earl of), L. R. (1895) 1 Q. B. 536	179
Sewell v. Burdick, L. R. 10 App. Ca. 74	56
Sheffield (Earl of) v. London Joint Stock Bank, L. R. 13 App. Ca. 333	4, 5, 11, 15, 17, 28

	PAGE
Simmons v. London Joint Stock Bank, L. R. (1891) 1 Ch. 270; App. Ca. (1892) 201 . . 4, 5, 6, 12, 13, 16, 19, 28, 31, 55	
Smith v. Virtue, 9 C. B. N. S. 214 156	
Solarte v. Palmer, 2 Cl. & F. 93 . . . . 163, 164, 165	
Stoessiger v. South Eastern Railway Co., 3 E. & B. 549 . . . 110	
Stoltz, *In re*, 6 Mod. 29 *See* ERRATUM 105	
TAYLOR v. Kymer, 3 B. & Ad. 320 . .	12
—— v. Trueman, M. & M. 453 .	12
Tweedle v. Atkinson, 1 B. & S. 393 .	68
WHISTLER v. Forster, 14 C. B. N. S. 248 .	. 8, 63, 174
Wookey v. Pole, 4 B. & Ald. 1 . .	. 31, 37
YOUNG v. Grote, 4 Bing. 253 .	176, 177, 178, 179, 180

ERRATA.

For *Re Stoltz*, p. 105, read *Buller* v. *Crips*.

After the word, *addresses*, in the last line of p. 116, *add* "or who accepts for the honour of the drawer, or one of the indorsers of the bill."

THE LAW

OF

NEGOTIABLE SECURITIES.

LECTURE I.

BEFORE proceeding to discuss the topics which await our consideration this evening, and for some evenings to come, I desire, by way of preface, with your permission, to state how it is that, almost at the close of my career and with the pressure of many engagements, I undertake a task which is generally committed to men of youthful brains, coming fresh from the study of law as a science in all its branches. My reasons are threefold. First, I was requested to undertake this task by Lord Justice Lindley. My reverent regard for him made me feel that his request was a command that must be obeyed. Next, I was glad to avail myself of an opportunity of discharging, if possible, some small portion of the debt which I owe to the four Inns of Court for having established, at the time when I came to the study of the law, a complete and effective system of legal education, and at a cost which brought it within the reach of men of the most moderate resources. Had those arrangements not been made, I should never have become a member of the Society of the Inner Temple, nor passed to the practice of a profession, in which I have met with greater rewards than I looked for, in which I have found kind and generous competitors, and have become familiarly acquainted with the great men, both in past times and in the present generation, who have built up the fabric of our commercial law. My third reason was, I desired to express my sympathy with the Legal Council of Education in its efforts to impart useful legal information, not only to lawyers, but to persons engaged in all departments of business.

With the consent of the Council of Legal Education, I have chosen a subject of the greatest importance to men engaged in commerce—a portion of law which is a monument of the practical skill and wisdom of the merchants of our land, and also of the courage, foresight, and prudence of our great Judges who turned mercantile usages into rules of law.

The subject I have selected has not been chosen for the purpose of making people litigious or conceited, nor with a view of depriving those who practise the law as a profession of opportunities of just and honourable employment. I shall be for the most part discussing transactions which are daily and hourly being carried out in the counting-houses of our land, whose nature, method, and character have been determined by law, and from which, although resting originally on mercantile usage, no departure is now permitted; transactions in which it is important to see whether those who are engaged in the actual commerce of the country are acting in conformity with the law; to see whether by present usage they have gone either in advance or fallen behind the rules which our Judges have laid down. I hope, by a simple exposition of the law, to enable men of business to understand more clearly the principles upon which their daily conduct rests, and I shall treat of a peculiar kind of property, without which the trade and commerce of this great Empire could never have exceeded the narrowest bounds. I am to speak of principles of law by which a vast and almost unparalleled system of credit has been established; of property that is most easily convertible and in respect to which the law for the most part is clear and simple; I am going to speak to you of property which lies at the mercy of any person in whose hands it may be placed; of property over which the utmost care should be exercised; of property which may be destroyed by the least neglect; of property in instruments, which may give rise to obligations even after they have been torn in pieces and those who made them deemed they no longer existed; of property which may be transferred with the utmost facility and acquired by every person who is a *bonâ fide* holder for value, although the true owner—mark this—has been no party directly, or indirectly, to the transaction.

A great French writer, in a preface to one of his books, says: "I am desirous of treating philosophy in a manner which is not philosophical," and I should like to say that, in treating the subject I have chosen, I desire to treat it in a manner which is not legal. I desire to treat it in a manner which will not be too dry for the man of business, nor yet too light for the members of the legal profession, whose presence here to-night I notice with pleasure. I desire you, however, to remember that I am going to deal with a portion of our law in which many words are used with a precise and definite meaning, and in the use of which that definite meaning should be ever present to the mind. There is such a tendency to drift away from clear, definite conceptions, that you and I must endeavour, in our use of technical words, to keep before our minds the exact meaning which the law has assigned them.

At the very outset of our study, then, we meet with the word "negotiable," and if we are to avoid mistake we must realize its exact meaning. After having been for many years in what may be called a liquid state it has had for nearly fifty years a rigid fixed meaning. If the things covered by legal technical words could be touched or handled, definition would be of little importance, but as they are not objects of sense but are purely intellectual, and exist only in the mind, a true and precise definition of them is of the utmost moment. I also lay greater stress on the importance of knowing the determinate ideas involved in the word "negotiable," and of your having present to your mind such determinate ideas whenever the word "negotiable" is used, because of the perils to which the Law of Negotiable Securities has been lately exposed. These perils arose from a forgetfulness of the meaning of the word "negotiable" and a misapprehension of the language of the Law Lords when dealing with a question of fact in the case of *The Earl of Sheffield* v. *The London Joint Stock Bank*, reported in Law Rep., 13 App. Cas. p. 333. These misapprehensions led to the judgment of Mr. Justice Kekewich in *Simmons* v. *The London Joint Stock Bank*, reported in Law Rep., 1891, 1 Chan., p. 270, and the decision of the Court of Appeal in the same case, reported in the same volume, p. 287. The House of Lords, as a judicial body, has not often rendered a greater service to the mercantile community than when it reversed both these decisions and thereby restored freedom and confidence to the transactions in negotiable securities in which our great bankers engage. Serious mischief, in my opinion, arises, from Judges stating too much when they are dealing only with questions of fact. It is an error common in the Chancery Division of this country. Baron Martin used to say, and I have heard him say it, that when a Judge is called upon either to state his finding of fact or an inference of fact, it would be well if he could state his finding without his reasons. The reasons of the Law Lords in the case of *The Earl of Sheffield* v. *The London Joint Stock Bank* in arriving at a conclusion of fact, gave rise to continued and expensive litigation in *Simmons* v. *The London Joint Stock Bank*, to which I have referred.

The reports of these two cases, involving altogether, I think, a hundred pages of reading, are taken up entirely with questions of fact; but, unfortunately, the statements of fact in *The Earl of Sheffield* v. *The London Joint Stock Bank* being regarded by Mr. Justice Kekewich as statements which were equivalent to legal propositions, the House of Lords had finally to say that the observations in *Earl of Sheffield* v. *The London Joint Stock Bank* were merely statements made in the course of finding conclusions of fact, and did not contain any principle of law at all. Neither *Simmons'* nor *Earl Sheffield's* case established a single principle of law. The law had been made clear and certain by decisions and the strict application of them when I came to its study nearly forty years ago.

These cases I must comment upon, because in any litigation in our Courts involving the question of negotiability, they are likely to be adduced, and unless carefully studied will probably cause you much perplexity. These cases have also been much considered in commercial circles, and it is of the utmost importance that the nature and effect of each decision should be rightly understood by men of business. *Earl Sheffield's case*, which is reported under the name of *Easton* v. *The London Joint Stock Bank* in 34 Chancery Division, p. 95, was tried before Mr. Justice Pearson. It is unfortunate that questions relating to commercial law should be determined otherwise than by a Judge and Jury. I am certain they could be disposed of in far less time by Judge and Jury than is occupied in the Chancery Division when such questions arise there. Mr. Justice Pearson simply decides a question of fact, and decides against Easton. In the same case, and reported in the same volume, the Court of Appeal dissents from the finding of fact of Mr. Justice Pearson, and itself finds a fact which in the view of the Court equally disentitles the plaintiff to recover. The plaintiff appeals to the House of Lords, and the House of Lords draws an entirely different inference of fact from either Mr. Justice Pearson or the Court of Appeal, and decides that the plaintiff was entitled to recover. In that case, unfortunately, the reasons of the Law Lords for arriving at their conclusion of fact were reported at great length. When *Simmons'* *case* came, as I have told you, before Mr. Justice Kekewich, he, regarding the observations of the Lords in arriving at a conclusion of fact as laying down legal propositions, decided in favour of Simmons. The case went by appeal to the Court of Appeal, and there the Court decided upon different grounds and reasons also in favour of Simmons; but in the House of Lords, L. R., App. Cases (1892), p. 201, by the firm application of legal principles, both these decisions were reversed, and the law of this country was brought back again to where it stood when I began to study the law, viz. that a negotiable instrument is one the property in which is acquired by any one who takes it *bonâ fide*, and for value, notwithstanding any defect of title in the person from whom he took it; from which it follows that an instrument cannot be negotiable unless it is such and in such a state that the true owner could transfer the contract or engagement contained therein by simple delivery of the instrument.

Now these are the two things to keep before your minds — (a) a "*negotiable*" instrument is one the property in which is acquired by every person who takes it *bonâ fide* and for value, (b) provided that the instrument is such and in that state that the true owner could transfer the contract or engagement contained therein by simple delivery of the instrument.

Now, the proposition just presented to you is a principle of law, and is the only statement I make to you with respect to the meaning of a negotiable instrument, and I hope you will never use the word "negotiable" except in the sense I have indicated. The definition I have given may not commend itself to all, and I feel it is open to some criticism. I have, however, always used it myself, and found it sufficiently accurate for all practical purposes. I believe, that by a careful examination of the language employed, "(a)" could be shown to involve "(b)," but I have put both into the definition to avoid all mistake. If one part of a definition can be said to be more important than another, "(a)" is more important than "(b)," yet in my conversation with students and young lawyers I have found them give me "(b)" as the definition of a negotiable instrument, omitting "(a)" altogether.

Then, remember whilst that is the principle of law, the question whether a man takes the instrument *bonâ fide* and for value, is a question of fact. The Court, as I shall show you hereafter, will decide as a matter of law whether an instrument is negotiable, except in the case where negotiability rests upon usage, but never forget that if the instrument is such and in such a state that some act other than delivery is required on the part of the true owner to pass the contract or engagement contained therein, it is not a negotiable instrument.

Let me show you by two illustrations the importance of keeping before your mind the nature of the instrument and its condition when considering the question of negotiability. For some years prior to 1886, Pennsylvanian Railroad certificates of shares when signed in blank were dealt in by English bankers and on the English Stock Exchange as negotiable instruments. It was supposed that the person who took them *bonâ fide* and for value acquired a perfectly good title to them irrespective of the title of the transferor. In the case of the *London and County Banking Co.* v. *The London and River Plate Bank*, reported in the Law Rep., Q. B. Div., vol. 20, p. 232, the question of their negotiability came up for judicial decision. On examining the instruments it was found by the terms appearing on the face of the instruments that the property in them could only pass by transfer on the face of the books of the company, and not by simple delivery. The Court held that notwithstanding the usage of the Stock Exchange and of Bankers, the instruments were not negotiable. They were not *such* that the property in them could pass by delivery.

Now let me call your attention to the importance of looking to the *state* of the instrument. You often talk of a bill of exchange as being negotiable. Well, that is perhaps, roughly speaking, true, but I tell you that a bill of exchange is not negotiable in all cases. If the property in the bill cannot be transferred except by the indorsement of the true owner, it is not negotiable because the property in it will not pass by mere delivery. You require another act of the true owner, viz., the writing of his name upon the instrument as well as delivery to pass the property in it.

This point will never be forgotten by you, if you study well the case of *Whistler* v. *Forster*, which will be found in the 14 Common Bench, New Series, page 248. Although that case relates to a cheque, its doctrine is applicable to a bill of exchange or promissory note. The simple forgetfulness to obtain the indorsement of the person in whose favour a cheque was drawn to order, deprived Mr. Whistler of the whole of the money that he gave for it.

Now, as I shall show you hereafter when I come to another part of my subject, whether a bill be drawn to the drawer's order or the order of a payee, or a cheque has been drawn to order, the property in that instrument can only pass by the drawer, or the payee, or the person in whose favour the cheque is drawn, putting his name on the back, and then delivering it with an intention to pass the property.

Now in *Whistler* v. *Forster* a cheque was drawn to the order of a payee. Whistler undoubtedly gave the payee full and complete value for the cheque, but in the transaction he forgot to get the signature of the payee, and consequently the property, according to mercantile law, had not passed to him. Before Whistler could get the signature of the payee to the cheque for the purpose of conveying the property—I need not tell you that if the transferor of a bill of exchange or cheque has not put his name to it, it is a perfectly good transaction if he puts his name subsequently, because, at all events, there is a past consideration, and it does not matter whether the consideration be past or present for the transfer of a negotiable instrument—before Whistler could get the signature of the payee, he received notice from the person who drew the cheque that the cheque had been obtained by the fraud of the person in whose favour it was drawn. At the trial it was established that there was fraud in procuring the cheque. It was found that Whistler had notice of the fraud before he got the signature of the payee. The Court held that the instrument was not *in such a state* when Whistler first received it without notice of the fraud as to give him a claim to it as a negotiable instrument; that Whistler could, therefore, have, according to the general principle of our law, no better title than that of the person with whom he dealt; that the person in whose favour the cheque was drawn, having no right himself because he had been guilty of a fraud in obtaining the cheque, Mr. Whistler, who cashed the cheque, had no right either. If, of course, he had got the signature of the person in whose favour the cheque was drawn before he had notice of the fraud, he then would have been a *bonâ fide* holder for value and would have had a perfect title. This case, and the preceding, therefore, are illustrations of a portion "(b)" of the definition above given, viz., that to be a negotiable instrument, the instrument must be such and in such a state that the true owner if he thought fit could pass the property in it by delivery.

Now, I am sorry to tell you that words are used so carelessly in conversation by many young men that they seem to think that the definition of a negotiable instrument is satisfied by saying, "Oh, a negotiable instrument is one the property in which passes by delivery from hand to hand." That is not the definition of a negotiable instrument. It may be and is an important element to consider, but it is far from satisfying the meaning of negotiability. And I am not sure, in many cases resting upon usage, whether people in the City have ever had their attention directed to this important part of negotiability, and the principal part of it, viz., the acquisition of the instrument by a person who takes it *bonâ fide* and for value, even although the true owner has neither by act nor deed been a party to the transaction, nor by his conduct conduced thereto.

Now let me put you on your guard. You must never fall into the error I have just indicated. I may impress the right view upon your minds by giving you illustrations of the way in which transferability by delivery has been confounded with negotiability. Just look at the case of *Rumball* v. *The Metropolitan Bank*, a case I shall have to refer you to, later on. It will be found in Law Reports, 2 Queen's Bench Division, p. 194. You will find that counsel arguing, mark you, in favour of the defendant who sought to assert his right to certain scrip for shares on the ground that they were negotiable, made his first point thus: First, he said, the scrip was, by virtue of usage, negotiable by delivery. If that means anything, it merely means that the scrip was, by usage, transferable by delivery. But when I am talking of *negotiability*, I am far beyond and outside the mere question of transferability and conveyance of property from man to man by delivery. This paper which I hold in my hand can be transferred by delivery. The property in a book may pass by delivery just as the property in many other articles that you may mention — clothes, tools of trade, and all the articles of commerce. But that doctrine does not assist you on the question of negotiability. Let anyone take my books to-night from my chambers and, except in market overt, sell them. If I can trace them, the person in whose possession they are, although he took them *bonâ fide* and for value, must surrender them to me, because the great principle of our law is that a man who is the true owner shall never cease to be the owner unless his act or conduct or lapse of time or forfeiture or bankruptcy, to speak generally, has deprived him of the property. But you and I are considering property which may be acquired irrespective of the act of the true owner. Again, in the case of *Earl of Sheffield* v. *The London Joint Stock Bank,* counsel arguing at the Bar of the Lords on behalf of the Bank (who claimed to retain instruments as being negotiable instruments taken *bonâ fide* and for value) presented the point as to negotiability thus: "The bonds held by the Bank were transferable by manual delivery, and were, therefore, negotiable securities." From transferability by delivery the inference of negotiability cannot be drawn. Counsel would have been nearly accurate if he had reversed the order and said the instruments were negotiable (stating the reasons why they were so), and therefore passed by delivery. Let me give you another illustration of the equivocal use of the word "negotiable." Take the statute-book of 1882, where you find the law of Bills of Exchange is codified. And very useful has been the codification, but the statute is a dead letter to our young men apart from open and liberal discussion, and I have known some of them, when I have had to examine them, by attempting to master portions of that code by mere act of memory, give useless and nonsensical answers. We need living discussion for such a measure as that of 1882; but if you look at it, you will find the phrase "negotiable by delivery" there used. That expression tends to mislead; it only means transferable by delivery; but, as I have told you, "transferable by delivery" is only one of the conditions of negotiability. The great element of negotiability is the acquisition of property by your own conduct, not by another's; that if you take it *bonâ fide* and for value, nobody can deprive you of it. Let me give you another illustration of the same error. Read again that case of *Easton* v. *The London Joint*

Stock Bank, to which I have already called your attention, before Mr. Justice Pearson, and see what is stated on page 96; you will read thus: "Evidence was given that the bonds were treated in the City of London as transferable from hand to hand." And to my surprise I find a Lord Justice saying that the evidence before Mr. Justice Pearson constituted the instruments negotiable. With all deference I say he was mistaken; such evidence does not constitute negotiability. To say that they are "transferable by delivery" is to say nothing perhaps with respect to *negotiability*. The other and principal element (a) must come first; and the second, (b) of course, I told you, must also be present in order that the instrument may be negotiable. Perhaps there are no cases in which the distinction between transferability by delivery and negotiability is so well seen or so distinctly marked as in the cases of *Taylor* v. *Trueman*, Moody and Malkin's Reports, p. 453, and *Taylor* v. *Kymer*, 3 Barnewall and Adolphus, p. 320.

Now, you will find in *Simmons' case* a most remarkable instance of forgetfulness of the true meaning of negotiability. I refer to it not for the purpose of disparaging illustrious counsel but of making you young men determined that whatever knowledge of law you possess it shall be exact. Let there be *no general impressions* within the domain of law. General impressions of a landscape may be all very well for an artist who wants to produce an effective picture, but absolute exactitude and certainty of expression and thought are essential in our profession. In *Simmons* v. *The London Joint Stock Bank* you will find that three most illustrious counsel actually thought that they got a sufficient admission to enable them to claim for their clients, the bankers, bonds which had been dealt with by a person having no authority to deal with them, by an admission that the bonds did pass from hand to hand by delivery; and when the case went from Mr. Justice Kekewich to the Court of Appeal those eminent counsel had to admit, though not to their discredit, because no man is wise at all hours, that they had made a mistake in accepting that admission ; and it was agreed that the argument should proceed upon the footing that not only did the instruments pass by delivery, but that the person who took them *bonâ fide* and for value would acquire a good title to them.

Now, of course, those of you who have the opportunity will read the two cases, *Earl of Sheffield* v. *The London Joint Stock Bank* and *Simmons* v. *The Same Bank*, and I trust you will find that I am justified in the whole of the criticisms I have offered with respect to them. The difficulties which arose in these cases could not have occurred when I first came to the Bar, because they could not arise at common law, where questions with respect to negotiable securities were then chiefly determined. A question of fact would have been tried by a jury, who gave no reasons for their findings : the question whether their verdict was against the weight of evidence could not have gone beyond the Court in which the action was commenced ; and as for reporting the evidence, as a rule it is unknown in our common law reports, except so far as it is necessary to set it forth for the purpose of seeing whether the direction of the judge was correct or whether there was evidence fit to be left to a jury ; nor did the judges presume to offer any observations when they directed a new trial; and so at the Common Law Bar we escaped the defect of a slavish adherence to opinions and statements of men in regard to facts in one case when dealing with the facts of another case. Deal with the facts in your own case ; know the principle of law applicable to them ; and you will advance then with confidence to the establishment or defence of your client's interests.

Now, I hope you understand, that if the instrument is such or in such a state that the true owner, if he desired to do so, could not pass the property in it by delivery, it is not a *negotiable* instrument; and although it is in such a state that the true owner could pass the property in it by delivery, it is not a *negotiable* instrument unless the rule of law relating to the instrument is this—that anybody who takes it *bonâ fide* and for value acquires a perfectly good title.

Now, let me pass to the consideration of a phrase in connection with our subject which I find in common use, and a phrase which I think may be misleading. I am sorry to find that so able a man as the late Lord Bowen should have given currency to it. You will find the expression in his judgment in *Easton* v. *London Joint Stock Bank*. His lordship there says: "Nevertheless a further question arises whether Lord Sheffield by the way he has treated these bonds has not estopped himself from denying their negotiability. If the negotiability of these bonds by estoppel so to speak arises. . . ." Of course such language could lead to no danger when used by so distinguished a judge, but I have heard people recently talk of negotiability by conduct and negotiability by estoppel, as if there were another distinct head of negotiability and a separate kind of estoppel. The negotiability of which I am speaking has nothing to do with the conduct of the true owner and nothing to do with the doctrine of estoppel. If you can rest your client's claim upon the negotiability of the instrument, you have nothing to do with conduct or estoppel or any such principle. The doctrine of estoppel may serve you if the property is not negotiable, but negotiability excludes the notion of any conduct on the part of the true owner. Title by estoppel is what men mean when they speak of negotiability by estoppel, but title by estoppel is a different thing altogether from negotiability, and you will find when I come hereafter to mention the case of *Goodwin* v. *Robarts*, how there the House of Lords put the claim of the bankers on two grounds, but both of them absolutely distinct—one that Goodwin was estopped by his conduct; the other that the instruments were negotiable, and having been taken by the bank *bonâ fide* and for value, they had a perfectly good title irrespective of the conduct of the plaintiff altogether.

Now, again I call your attention to another error, the error of supposing that the doctrine of constructive notice enters into the consideration of the meaning of *bona fides* when we speak of a *bonâ fide* holder. Until recently, I never heard a suggestion that it did. I am sure it is a doctrine that has been quite unknown to the Courts of Common Law for forty years. But since the decision of the House of Lords in *Earl of Sheffield* v. *London Joint Stock Bank*, it has become more frequent to hear intelligent lawyers say that a *bonâ fide* holder of a negotiable instrument may be affected with constructive notice of a limited authority or of misconduct on the part of the person transferring the instrument. There can be no doubt that in some of the judgments of the Law Lords in that case there are expressions that seem to give ground for such an opinion. Thus Lord Bramwell used these words: "I have used the expression 'notice of the infirmity of the title,' but I wish to guard against the notion that I think it precise and accurate: nor would it be right to say 'notice that possibly the pledgor had no power to pledge as he did,' because that is always possible and the expression should be something like this: 'Notice of the infirmity of the pledgor's title or of such facts and matters as made it reasonable that inquiry should be made into such title.'" Lord Macnaghten said: "If the bankers relied upon Mozley's representations, it turns out now that in this case his representations were not well founded, and as loss has occurred the loss must fall on those who trusted without inquiring into the representations which he made." These expressions may be justifiable, because in the *Earl of Sheffield* v. *London Joint Stock Bank*, the claim of the defendants was rested, among other things, on the ground of their being legal holders of the instruments by the authorised act of the agent of Lord Sheffield without any notice of such agent having exceeded his authority in raising the amount of money he did on the instruments committed to his care. It may well be that where a beneficial interest is sought to be destroyed by the possession of the legal estate without notice, the person setting up the legal estate may be constructively affected with notice of the beneficial interest. But in the case of negotiable instruments the *bonâ fide* holder does not claim them by virtue of any estate or interest created by the true owner, but by virtue of his having taken the instruments honestly and for value. If he honestly relied upon misrepresentations and honestly abstained from making inquiries and took the instrument without suspicion of any wrong being committed, he has in my opinion a perfectly good title to the instrument. The question is not whether the person who took the instrument *ought* to have suspected but whether he *did* suspect, and I believe the view I am now presenting has been recognized by the decision of the House of Lords in *Simmons* v. *London Joint Stock Bank*. In considering whether a man is a *bonâ fide* holder you are to determine what knowledge he had, not what knowledge he might or ought to have had or what inquiries he ought to have made. You are to determine what was the state of *his* mind; not what would have been under the circumstances the state of another person's mind, or what course another person would have pursued. This, I believe, is the true rule, whether the person deciding the question of fact be a judge or juryman. When you have read *Simmons' Case* as reported in the House of Lords you will see with what difficulty we have escaped this error of constructive notice, and the House of Lords, I am certain, will save transactions in negotiable securities from any such danger in the future. There is nothing that speaks so much for the honesty of men engaged in commerce as this doctrine of negotiability. So seldom does any wrong arise in connexion with such instruments, that the great merchants of this and other countries have thought that it is better to suffer an occasional loss than embarrass, by unnecessary inquiries, transactions which must be carried through rapidly. It is the merchants of the City of London who in this country have created property with this particular incident.

Now, understand me, we have nothing to do with constructive notice in determining who is a *bonâ fide* holder. How our equity friends have lived on constructive notice! Strike that doctrine out of their books, and what would become of them? The equity judges no doubt have rendered great services. I may, in passing, remind you of the creation of equitable assets, and the separate estate of married women; the right of redemption of estates forfeited at law, and of a valid mortgage by deposit of title deeds. But into this domain of negotiability I am certain the House of Lords will never allow constructive notice to enter, nor yet the doctrine that a person who takes a negotiable instrument is bound to make inquiries. A person who takes a negotiable instrument is not *bound* to make any inquiry: if, however, he refrains from asking questions because he suspects there is something wrong, he is not an honest holder. He is bound to be honest; if he suspects the honesty of the person with whom he is dealing he is bound to withdraw from the transaction unless the suspicion is removed. You must not forget, however, that if the holder for value of a negotiable instrument took it with *actual* notice that the person with whom he was dealing had only a limited interest therein, for example, as pledgee, the holder of the instrument, whatever may be the advance he made upon it, and however honestly he may have acted in so doing, cannot acquire a greater interest in it than that which the person with whom he dealt could lawfully transfer. (See *Earl of Sheffield's case*.) I believe in the vast majority of cases in which negotiable instruments are dealt with, men on both sides of the transaction are honest; and when professionally I have had to do with disputed questions as to bills of exchange, they have generally been in connexion with outside men who were willing to take commercial bills in the Strand at half price, not transactions among the merchants, bill-brokers, and bankers in the City. Transactions in negotiable securities must be passed through rapidly: there is no time for thinking, except as to the terms on which the bills shall be discounted or purchased: no constructive notice, no speculations as to what answers would have been given if inquiry had been made, can be allowed to affect them. This would be the direction of a judge as I have heard it at common law in a dispute between a person claiming the instrument as a *bonâ fide* holder for value and a person once the owner and who, if the claim is not established, is still the owner. "Gentlemen of the jury, take all the circumstances of the case into your consideration: the absence of inquiry, the nature and extent of the consideration which was given, the character and position of the person with whom the plaintiff dealt, the apparent carelessness with which the transaction was conducted, and if you are of opinion that this plaintiff, notwithstanding his carelessness, notwithstanding that he made no inquiries, honestly believed that the man with whom he was dealing was acting properly, find your verdict for the plaintiff here who claims the instruments. If, on the other hand, you think that the plaintiff had the slightest suspicion that the man with whom he was dealing was acting improperly, and that suspicion was not removed but was upon his mind when the transaction was carried through, notwithstanding he gave value for the instruments, find your verdict for the defendant who in such case is still the owner." It would be utterly wrong to say, "Gentlemen, if you think the plaintiff was careless in taking the instrument, find your verdict for the true owner;" or, "If you think there were facts brought to the knowledge of the plaintiff which should have led him to make inquiry, and such inquiry would have shewn that the transferor was acting dishonestly, find your verdict for the true owner." And excuse my saying that I think the following observations of Mr. Justice Kekewich in *Simmons' Case* are not well founded. He said: "If this decision renders it more difficult for dishonest brokers to deal with securities by pledging those of a client to secure an advance to themselves, the law will not be open to blame nor will there be occasion to regret the result. On the other hand, honest brokers will not be in any way impeded, for their title will be good, and they will have no real difficulty in persuading the banks of that fact." The law would, in my opinion, in respect of such instruments as we are considering, be very much to blame if it merely put difficulties in the way of dishonest brokers. The law should be framed, and I believe has been framed, to protect people who, acting honestly, take such instruments for value in the course of their business. To frame the law for the purpose suggested by the learned judge would nearly destroy business altogether. It is no use considering whether an honest broker could easily, or not, show his honesty. We are to consider not what a broker, honest or dishonest, has to do, but what a person, who buys such instruments and advances money upon them daily, has to do. *He* is to act honestly and to deal only with people who he believes are acting honestly. "Why should not the broker satisfy the banker of his true position?" Why, in the terror of a panic or in times of great demand for money, bill-brokers and stock-brokers who deal in these things come in and want money in a moment. To delay the application for a minute might lead to the bankruptcy of an important house, and to other and most serious consequences. These are transactions to be carried through with marvellous rapidity. I do not expound the principle of negotiability at this length in order that a dishonest man may avail himself of it to cheat and defraud, but that a true and honest man may know how he is protected by the law of his country.

As to cases in this part of our law, do not trouble yourselves with reading many: select the weightiest and best. Read and study them; but when you have studied them, for Heaven's sake, rise with a clear principle that you can enunciate, so that when you proceed into court you can tell the judge what your principle is, and the case which sustains it; and if he mentions the case you can answer him with your principle.

Now, there is one case on the question of *bona fides* which is delightful reading—I mean the case of *Raphael* v. *The Bank of England*—reported in 17 Common Bench Reports, p. 162. The action was brought to recover from the Bank of England the amount of a bank-note for £500. The plaintiffs were money dealers in London, and they sued upon the title of Victor St. Paul & Co., money-changers, of Paris. It appeared that some bank-notes had been stolen, and one of them was the note in respect of which the action was brought. The payment of the stolen notes was immediately stopped, and notice of the stealing of these notes, with a list of them, had been given to nearly all the money-changers in Paris, and among other people to Victor St. Paul & Co. It was proved to be the practice of that house to file all notices of stolen notes served upon them. On a certain day a man comes in and asks Mr. Victor St. Paul to change a Bank of England note for him. There behind him was the list of stolen bank-notes. A glance at it would have protected the true owner at whose instance the Bank of England had stopped payment of the note. Mr. Victor St. Paul stated at the trial that he did not look at the file and had no recollection of the notice. Mr. Victor St. Paul at once cashed the note, giving for every sovereign 24 francs 95 cents., being the course of exchange on the day in question. He sent the note to Raphael in England, who demanded payment at the Bank of England. Payment was refused, and in the action the Bank of England pleaded that Victor St. Paul was not a *bonâ fide* holder for value, and that he was not a holder without notice of the theft. It is curious to remark what happened at the trial. Chief Justice Jervis put certain questions to the jury, which they answered. They found that Victor St. Paul & Co. did give value for the note, that they had notice of the robbery, that they had no knowledge of the loss at the time they took the note, but they had the means of knowledge if they had properly used it, and that they took the note *bonâ fide*. Upon these findings the learned judge said: "That will be a verdict for the plaintiff." Then, apparently, some of the jurymen, not liking the notion that a careless holder should recover, endeavoured to assist the Bank of England in obtaining a new trial by making affidavits saying that if they had known that the plaintiff was to have the verdict they would not have given the answers they did. On the motion for a new trial the Court allowed, against the current of decisions, the affidavits to be read. The counsel moving stated that the affidavits shewed that six of the jury did not concur in the verdict as entered. The Chief Justice: "What do the jurymen say?" On one of the affidavits being read the Chief Justice Jervis said in his severest manner, "A man who could make out such an affidavit as that is utterly unfit to be a juryman." The Court refused to grant a rule, being of opinion that the Chief Justice upon the findings, had rightly directed the verdict to be entered for the plaintiff.

Now, what did that case settle? That a man who takes a note or bill of exchange honestly and truly for value, although he had the means at his command of determining whether the note or bill was one that he ought to take, but for the moment forgot to use those means, is entitled to assert himself to be the true owner, and to assert his right in the instrument against every other person. Read that case diligently. It put an end to a whole series of cases in which judges had been saying that if a man takes a bill of exchange carelessly and not in such a way as a prudent man would have taken it, he could not recover although he took it honestly and for value. Since the decision in that case, that doctrine has been completely destroyed. You will find the cases to which I refer in the Report of *Raphael* v. *The Bank of England*. You need not read them except for the instruction to be derived from examining the errors of great minds. The carelessness of the person who claims the instrument must be considered in coming to the conclusion of his *bona fides*; but when once you come to the conclusion, having regard to all the circumstances, that he took the instrument *bonâ fide* and for value, he is entitled to the instrument and to all the rights under it notwithstanding his carelessness, notwithstanding he made no inquiry, notwithstanding he was informed of facts which would have led a reasonable mind to make further inquiry.

Now, let me, before I conclude this evening's address, just call your attention to the question of consideration. Now, you often hear a great deal that is inexact in respect to consideration. You will find in the books the expression "full consideration," sometimes "*adequate* consideration." I tell you that if the tribunal that has to try the question whether the claimant is a *bonâ fide* holder for value of a negotiable instrument comes to the conclusion that he took it honestly and for value, however small that value, he is entitled to the property in the instrument. But let me not be misunderstood. There is no criterion so useful for the purpose of determining the *bona fides* of the person who takes a negotiable instrument as the price he pays for it. Watch my words, "if the tribunal comes to the conclusion that he took it *bonâ fide*, and for value," then although the value may be inadequate, he is entitled to the property in the instrument; but before the tribunal comes to that conclusion it will seriously consider the consideration that was given; it will give due weight to the inadequacy of the price that was paid. Sometimes the inadequacy of the price may leave no doubt that the bill was not taken in good faith; sometimes the adequacy of the consideration will be alone sufficient to establish *bona fides*. Hence, of course, Chief Justice Jervis, as any sensible man would do, the moment he found that Victor St. Paul in Paris gave exactly the full amount in French money for the £500 note, had no doubt whatever that at the time when Victor St. Paul parted with his money he believed that he was getting a good and valid instrument; or in other words, he believed the man was acting honestly in getting the note changed. If he did, if that was his state of mind, then he was entitled to recover. In former days it did not take Baron Martin, with his practical skill, long to dispose of some of these cases; and now I see they take, in equity, five days to try. Let me tell you what I once witnessed before him, and thereby became impressed with the importance of the consideration given, in considering whether a man took an instrument *bonâ fide*. A case was called on in a court crowded with barristers, who had heard that an interesting and intricate fraud in connection with a bill of exchange was to be unfolded. The case was opened, and the counsel for the plaintiff stated that evidence of fraud on the part of the person who transferred the instrument to his client would cast upon him the burthen of showing that his client took the instrument *bonâ fide* and for value; that he should content himself with proving the signature of the defendant—the only matter, at present, on which he had to supply proof; and that after evidence of the fraud had been offered by the defendant, he should show that his client discounted the bill at a very moderate rate, he having given for the bill of £200 the sum of £197.

Mr. Baron Martin at once said: "If that be so, why trouble yourself about burthen of proof. Let us see *your man!*" The plaintiff was accordingly put into the box. He produced his cheque for £197, payable to the order of the man who transferred the bill. The cheque shewed that it had been paid by his bankers, and in his pass-book he was debited by them with the amount. He stated he had parted with all the money the cheque represented, that he had no notice of any misconduct, and had no suspicion that the man who transferred the bill to him was acting dishonestly. He was cross-examined by defendant's counsel, without anything arising to cast a doubt upon the evidence given in chief.

Baron Martin then said to the counsel for defendant: "I suppose you are not going to call the man who committed the fraud on your client, to give an account different from that the plaintiff has given." "No, my lord; how can I, with any advantage? I could only produce him as a disgraced man," said the counsel for defendant. "Quite right," said the judge. "I don't see how you can. Have you any evidence at all to show that what the plaintiff has said is untrue?" "None," was the reply. "Then, if you like, you can address the jury upon the question whether they believe the account which the plaintiff has given of the transaction." Before the defendant's counsel could say whether he would address the jury or not, they intimated, through their foreman, that they believed the plaintiff's story.

Baron Martin thereupon said: "I will ask the jury whether they believe the plaintiff took the bill honestly, or whether he gave £197 for the instrument with a suspicion of there being any dishonesty, which if brought home to him would make the instrument in his hands a bit of waste paper?" The jury said they believed that the plaintiff took the bill honestly. With that Baron Martin said: "Gentlemen, you may now find your verdict for the plaintiff for the full amount of the bill, without troubling yourselves whether there was any fraud committed on the defendant or not." The crowd of barristers soon dispersed, all of them leaving the court admiring the practical sagacity and business energy of the great judge.

Now let me offer to you some few suggestions which may be useful to you in dealing with the question of *bonâ fides*. If ever you should be in a case such as that I have just described, always ask yourselves first of all, What is the value of the instrument that the claimant says he took *bonâ fide?* and secondly, What is the consideration that he gave for it? The disproportion between the value of the bill and the amount given may supply cogent evidence of dishonesty. If, of course, the instrument is worth nothing—and there are plenty of men, unfortunately, who put their names on bills of exchange who do not, by the ink they put there, add the slightest value to the instrument—the smallness of the consideration will not help you. If a bill for £100 at three months is a good commercial bill, readily discountable in the City for three or four per cent. per annum, and the claimant gave £50 for it, knowing the character and value of the bill, the jury will have very little difficulty in coming to the conclusion that the man who took the bill must have known perfectly well that the man with whom he was dealing was not acting honourably or had not come by the bill honestly. There is another thing with respect to *bona fides* which I must mention. It is not necessary to shew that the man who took the negotiable instrument knew the exact wrong that was being committed. The great principle of negotiability is guarded by the practical rule that no man shall be deemed a *bonâ fide* owner of a negotiable instrument in respect of which he had a *suspicion* at the time he took it that there was something wrong on the part of the person with whom he was dealing.

Now, you will find the definition of *bona fides* and the doctrine that inadequacy of consideration may be evidence of dishonesty well stated in a judgment of Lord Blackburn in the case of *Jones* v. *Gordon*, 2 Appeal Cases, 676. He tells you there that in criminal cases the general evidence that is given to shew that the receiver of goods which were stolen knew that they were stolen is, that he has given a great undervalue for them, and that in like manner if it is shewn that a considerable undervalue was given for bills, it is an important element in considering whether the man who gave that undervalue was acting *bonâ fide*. Then he goes on to tell you, in that simple but forcible language which made him the great instructor of those who had the privilege to hear him, that if he has given an undervalue, but done it honestly in a blundering, stupid way, yet he is entitled to claim the instrument as his own. Therefore the extent of the consideration is most important in determining the question of *bona fides*. It is not necessary that it should be full; it is necessary that there should be some; and the Courts will not inquire into the nature and extent of the consideration. But the amount of the consideration may be of the most vital importance in determining whether the man has taken the instrument *bonâ fide* and for value. If he has not given consideration, if it is a gift, he cannot claim it as against the true owner who has been defrauded. If he has given a sovereign for the bill he is entitled to it, if he has taken it honestly —if, considering all the circumstances, and the fact that he paid *only* the sovereign, you still come to the conclusion that he took it honestly. Where a person advances money on account of a negotiable instrument, and seeks to retain it only for the money actually advanced, if the tribunal is assured of the actual advance of the money, it is difficult, in the absence of direct and cogent evidence of bad faith, to come to any other conclusion than that the person making the advance took the instrument *bonâ fide*. If the consideration for the transfer of a bill of exchange be a past consideration, as for a debt already existing, the inquiry into the *bona fides* of the transferee may involve great care. If the debt is owing to a banker who may frequently have customers whose accounts are overdrawn and whose customers bring cheques for large amounts in reduction of an overdrawn account, in the absence of other evidence of bad faith, there is no reason why the transaction should not be readily accepted as an honest one. If, however, a bill of exchange is taken for a private debt or for a debt owing to a man who dabbles in discounting paper, as the creditor is not worse off by taking the bill for a past debt, he is parting with nothing, and may have the chance of getting a debt paid which perhaps would not be otherwise paid, the following inquiries suggest themselves. What is the amount of the debt? is it large or small? how long has it been owing? has the transferor made any recent appreciable reduction of it? has the transferor to the knowledge of the transferee had the opportunity of obtaining suddenly a bill of exchange for services rendered or any business transaction? did the transferee make any inquiries as to how the transferor came by the bill? The importance of these inquiries is seen when I tell you that in a case within my own experience, where the debt due to the transferee was £250, that it had been outstanding twelve months, that the transferor had been pressed for payment and had written more than once to say that it was quite out of his power then to pay the debt, that the transferee on having the bill offered in satisfaction of the debt made no enquiries as to how the debtor came by it, the jury, doubtless thinking that the transferee abstained from asking questions lest he should be deprived of the chance of getting his debt paid by reason of the answers which might be given, found that although the plaintiff took the bill for value, he did not take it *bonâ fide*. If the transferee should say he did make inquiries, always ask what they were, because the answers may be just as useful in shewing the want of *bona fides* as the absence of inquiry itself.

Now, in my opinion the next thing which it is most

important for you to consider and bear in mind is this, that it does not matter at all who the person is with whom you deal, if you take the instrument *bonâ fide* and for value. Therefore, if he is an agent, what does it matter? If you take negotiable instruments from a man whom you know to be an agent, believing he has authority to deal with them in the way he is doing, although he is acting most fraudulently in the disposition of the bills, you are entitled to them.

I am in this connexion again led to remind you of the cases of *Sheffield* v. *The London Joint Stock Bank* and *Simmons* v. *The London Joint Stock Bank*, as they are reported in the House of Lords. In the case of *Sheffield* v. *The London Joint Stock Bank*, the Law Lords said : " We come to the conclusion that the bank officials, when they took the instruments, knew that the person from whom they took them was not the owner and had only a limited interest therein." They, therefore, held that Lord Sheffield was entitled to redeem his securities on paying the sum of money he had authorized to be raised on them. In *Simmons* v. *London Joint Stock Bank* the House of Lords arrived at the conclusion that the bank officials, although they knew they were dealing with an agent, yet honestly believed that the agent had authority to pledge the securities in the manner and to the extent arranged. They held that the bank had a perfectly good title to the securities. The decisions of the House of Lords in *Sheffield* v. *The London Joint Stock Bank* and *Simmons* v. *The same Bank* are not, as is sometimes supposed, in actual conflict, but perfectly consistent with each other. Once affect a holder for value of negotiable securities with notice that the person from whom he took them was not the owner of them, but had only a limited interest therein, then such holder, however honestly he may have acted in taking the securities, will acquire no other interest in them than that which the person with whom he dealt could lawfully transfer. But if the holder for value deal with an agent, honestly believing that the agent has full and ample authority to deal with the negotiable instruments in the way he is doing, whether by sale or pledge, then such holder is entitled to retain the instruments either as owner or pledgee, and to assert the complete or partial ownership of them, notwithstanding the fraud on the true owner which the agent may have committed. You must unfortunately read the two cases to which I have referred—two cases which will give you the trouble of reading a hundred pages of discussion of fact. The principles of law applied in those cases have been recognised as principles of law for well nigh fifty years.

My first lecture, you will see, has been concerned with the ascertainment of the meaning of a *negotiable* instrument, which it is essential for everybody to know in business—ay, perhaps more important in business than to the lawyer, because the lawyer may only seldom be called upon to advise. Still, never forget, it is the privilege of a lawyer not to measure his studies by the necessities of professional employment, but to open his mind to the mastery, if possible, of the law in all its various departments. Men of business, it is important that you should know the meaning of negotiability, in order to take care of the instruments themselves—in order to see that you do not suffer either by failure to give notice of dishonour, or by failure to take the signature of the transferor, because you can only sue persons on bills of exchange who put their names on them. It is important that you should know all about these instruments, their value, and nature; and to the lawyer it may be equally important to have listened to my address on this first great question of the meaning of negotiability, although I know I shall only have recalled to his recollection the results of previous study.

Now with these observations I thank you for your attendance and your patient and encouraging hearing, and next time, if you will come and see me, I will tell you what instruments are comprised under the head of "Negotiable Securities."

LECTURE II.

I suppose that almost every lecturer is subject to misapprehension. It has been said that on the last occasion upon which I had the honour and privilege to speak to you I told you that a negotiable instrument was one which could *only* be acquired by a *bonâ fide* purchaser for value. I can only say that I did not intend to say anything of the kind, and as I told you that a Bank of England note was a negotiable instrument, and as most of you, I hope, have received a present of such an instrument from the true owner, you do not need to be told that the true owner of a negotiable instrument has all the powers of the owner of any other property. But the incident and attribute of the property that we are considering is, that although the true owner may dispose of it by gift *inter vivos*, by *donatio mortis causâ*, or by will, or in any other way the law permits, yet he may lose it by some person taking it, either from a finder or a thief, *bonâ fide* and for value, and thereby becoming the owner.

As there may be some present to-night who were not present at the last lecture, I will state shortly its results. I stated that a negotiable instrument was one the property in which is acquired by a person who takes it *bonâ fide* and for value, the instrument being in that state that the true owner, if he wished to part with the property in it, could pass it by delivery. I told you also that it did not matter whether, in a case of a negotiable instrument, a person purchased the instrument or advanced money upon it; that in the former case he became the owner, and in the latter case could detain the instrument until his advance was repaid. In *Simmons* v. *The London Joint Stock Bank* an objection was taken that a person who advanced money upon a negotiable instrument did not acquire a title to the extent of the advance. Lord Herschell, with his native vigour, reasoned to the conclusion that he did, notwithstanding that no authority was given to him for the proposition. I would like to call your attention to the case of *Wookey* v. *Pole*, 4 Barnewall & Alderson, p. 1, which establishes the proposition that a person who advances money upon a negotiable instrument obtains a perfectly good title to the extent of his advance. You will there see the difference at Common Law between a pledge of personal chattels by an agent authorized to sell them and the pledge of an agent authorized to sell negotiable securities. In the former case the pledgee acquired no right to retain the goods: in the latter he acquired a right to retain the negotiable securities to the extent of the advance. It therefore makes no difference whether the person who takes the instrument *bonâ fide* takes it acquiring the whole by purchase or by making an advance upon it.

The next thing I dealt with was, What is the meaning of *bona fides* when one speaks of a *bonâ fide* holder? I am afraid that here also I have been misunderstood, because some persons who listened to me last week have said that, with respect to a negotiable instrument, the question is whether the person who took the instrument ought not to have suspected that the man who was parting with the instrument had no title or was acting dishonestly. I told you (and I hope that you will correct me if I am wrong, and I should like to spend an evening in which to put right the mistakes that I commit) that it is not the question in the case of negotiable instruments whether the man who takes them ought to have suspected dishonesty or whether he acted rationally, or acted as other reasonable men would. The sole question, in my opinion, is the state of his mind. Did he take it honestly although he took it stupidly and in a blundering and irrational manner? If you answer the question that he took it *bonâ fide*, then he is entitled to claim and to retain the property, notwithstanding his blundering, and notwithstanding his stupidity. But if, on the other hand, upon looking at the whole of the circumstances, you should come to the conclusion (as I told you), that he suspected that there was something wrong, then he cannot claim the property as having been taken by him *bonâ fide* and for value. Another thing which I guarded you against was this. I said that it would be a great mistake if the doctrine of constructive notice, or that there were facts which ought to lead a man to make enquiry, was applied to negotiable instruments, which pass with marvellous rapidity, and under circumstances of necessity in this great city. But I told you that if it was a case of conflicting equities where the legal estate had been conveyed by the authority of the true owner, then, of course, it appeared to me that as equity has always taken care to guard the beneficial interest, it might be that in such case a question would arise whether there was not really constructive notice with regard to the authority of the person with whom he was dealing, or whether upon the facts disclosed he ought not to have made further enquiry.

Having said so much I am going to pass on now to perhaps the most important matter that can engage the attention of lawyers. What is now about to engage our attention is the list of negotiable securities. I have discussed with you what a negotiable security is. I want to-night to give you the list of them, and in so doing I must at once draw your attention to the important distinction between instruments and contracts which, made in England, have their nature, incidents and effects defined and regulated by English law, and contracts and instruments which are created in foreign countries. Unless, gentlemen, you realize the distinction between those two you will not act with safety in your business transactions nor be competent to advise persons who may desire your guidance in matters relating to negotiable securities.

First of all will you take this from me, and I believe it to be correct, that with respect to instruments that are made in this country and to which the law of England is applicable, instruments created here by either individuals or companies, the element of negotiability cannot be added to them either by stipulation or by usage. That is the first thing that you have to learn—that the element of negotiability cannot be added to such instruments by any usage whatever. The question, whether an English instrument is negotiable, is a question of law to be determined by the judge, and if he is satisfied that it is a negotiable instrument he is to hear no evidence to the contrary. If it is not in his opinion a negotiable instrument, he is to refuse to hear all evidence of usage to shew that it is, however long that usage may have been continued. In short, the list of negotiable securities coming into existence under English law is closed, until the Legislature itself annexes the incident of negotiability to some fresh instruments. This doctrine is established by two or three cases to which I desire to call your attention. The first is *Grant* v. *Vaughan* in the 3rd Burrows, page 1516, in which Lord Mansfield distinctly lays it down that the question, whether an instrument is a negotiable instrument or security, is a question of law to be determined by the judge. Hence, if you look at *Edie* v. *The East India Company* which you will find reported in 2 Burrows, page 1216, you will find there that Lord Mansfield laid it down that it having been once judicially decided that an instrument was negotiable, he was wrong in allowing evidence of usage to show that it was not, and on his attention being called to the earlier decision on a motion for a new trial he declared that he was mistaken at the trial in allowing evidence of the usage, and that there ought to be a new trial. That is to say in *Grant* v. *Vaughan* he held clearly and distinctly, apparently for the first time, that a cheque payable to " Bearer " was a negotiable instrument, and that the man who took it honestly and for value either from a thief or a finder could sue the person who drew it. In *Edie* v. *The East India Company* there was an indorsement to an individual without saying "or order." I shall discuss indorsement when I come to treat of bills of exchange. But let me assume this amount of knowledge at present—that a bill of exchange may be indorsed to A. B. Evidence was admitted to show that according to the usage of merchants, such an indorsement was a restrictive indorsement and that A. B. could not pass the property in the bill of exchange by an indorsement of it. Lord Mansfield admitted the evidence, but found that he had made a mistake in so doing because by a decision previously given it had been laid down that such an indorsement was not restrictive. He directed that a new trial should be had and laid down the doctrine that the law having determined the nature of the instrument, no evidence of usage was admissible to show that the instrument possessed a nature or quality different from that which the law ascribed to it.

Now comes a case which I trust you will read. Do not take its supposed effect from a text-book. Read the case for yourselves.

I too often find men carrying about with them scraps from text-books, and think they are sufficiently furnished for an examination or their profession. They are greatly mistaken; they may and should read text-books, but above all let them read and study the reports of decided cases. It was my custom, when I attended classes, to take a list of the cases given to me by the lecturers to the admirable library of the society of which I was a member, and there to read and study for myself the cases to which my attention had been called. Now there is one case on which the distinction I am presenting clearly rests. The case is *Crouch* v. *The Crédit Foncier Company* of England, reported in the Law Reports, 8 Queen's

Bench, page 374. I ask you to read, mark, learn, and inwardly digest it. In it you have the considered judgment of the Court of Queen's Bench delivered by that most remarkable man, Lord Blackburn. From the facts stated in the case it appeared that the Crédit Foncier Company had under its seal issued certain instruments which were called debentures, by which they promised to pay to the bearer £100 with interest. There was a covenant, however, to pay the debenture according to certain drawings. The defendants sold ten debentures for £100 each to a person named Macken. Macken never parted with these debentures, but his house was broken into and the ten debentures were stolen therefrom. Crouch took one of them from the thief *bonâ fide* and for value. The company at the instance of Macken refused to pay this debenture to the plaintiff. It was tacitly admitted at the trial that similar documents were in practice treated as negotiable. A verdict was found for the plaintiff, leave being reserved to move to enter the verdict for the defendants. A rule nisi was obtained pursuant to the leave, and after argument the Court held that the rule to enter a verdict for the defendants should be made absolute. Mr. Justice Blackburn most carefully examined the whole of the facts in order to see whether in any aspect of them the instrument could be held to be negotiable. He decided first, that being under seal it could not be a promissory note, and therefore was not a negotiable instrument under the head of promissory notes. He found further that it contained promises outside the promise to pay money which in itself prevented it from being a negotiable security or a negotiable instrument. He stated the general rule of the law of England to be that an owner of property does not hold it on a precarious title liable to be divested if a thief or finder could find a *bonâ fide* purchaser, and that it is not within the competency of private persons either by contract or usage to attach such an incident to any property. Such an incident may be annexed by statute or by the law merchant, but in no other way can it be added to an English instrument made in England. A stipulation between obligor and obligee that the obligor may pay to any one who holds the instrument is perfectly good, and such a payment would be good as against the obligee, but such a stipulation falls far short of negotiability. He therefore held that a debenture of a public company existing under English law is not a negotiable instrument, and that the plaintiff was not entitled to recover, notwithstanding the usage of the English market, by which such an instrument was treated as negotiable. You will have no difficulty, I think, if you will study these cases, in coming to a conclusion as to what are negotiable instruments with respect to instruments created and arising on English territory.

The cases of *Gorgier* v. *Mieville*, and *Goodwin* v. *Robarts*, to which your attention will be called later on, are perfectly consistent with *Crouch* v. *Crédit Foncier Co.*, because in the former cases the instruments were decided to be instruments arising under foreign and not English law. Mr. Justice Blackburn would, in my view, have certainly acquiesced in the decision in *Goodwin* v. *Robarts*. I do not think the observations of Cockburn, C.J., in *Goodwin* v. *Robarts* when that case was before the Exchequer Chamber, have affected in any degree the binding effect of *Crouch* v. *The Crédit Foncier Company*.

There is one case to which I must call your attention—the case of *Rumball* v. *The Metropolitan Bank*, which is in the Law Reports, 2 Queen's Bench Division, page 194—in which it was held that scrip certificates of the Anglo-Egyptian Banking Company, an English company, which entitled the bearer to be registered as the holder of shares after making certain payments, were by the usage of the English market negotiable. This case seems to be in direct opposition to *Crouch* v. *The Crédit Foncier Company*, and if not directly overruled, has been so adversely commented upon as to entitle me to say that at this day I do not think that *Rumball* v. *The Metropolitan Bank* would receive acceptance in the Court of Appeal or the House of Lords.

Assuming *Crouch* v. *The Crédit Foncier Company* to be a binding authority, let me tell you now, as far as I can, what are the instruments which are negotiable by the law of England. I am speaking now of English instruments. First of all, then, bills of exchange, promissory notes, Bank of England notes, the notes of country bankers, cheques—but all with this condition, that they are in such a state that the true owner, if he so desired, could pass the property in them by delivery. If they are not in a state by which the true owner can pass the property in them by a simple act of delivery, with intention to convey the property, the documents are not negotiable instruments. Do not forget that I gave you a case in point on the last occasion, *Whistler* v. *Forster*, in the 14th Common Bench, New Series, which shewed the importance of this very doctrine, and the loss which a man may incur in consequence of not having the instrument endorsed to him by the person from whom he takes it.

The next is Exchequer Bills. If you want to see the form of exchequer bills you can find it in the case of *Wookey* v. *Pole*, in 4 Barnewall & Alderson, page 1, or in the case of *Brandao* v. *Barnett*, which can be found in the 12th Clarke & Finnelly, page 787. You must look at the form of it. It begins by saying: "This bill entitles ——— or order to one thousand pounds and interest after the rate of two pence halfpenny per diem payable out of the first aids or supplies to be granted in the next session of parliament. If the blank is not filled up this bill will be paid to bearer." Take the exchequer bill without any name in it and it passes like a bill of exchange or a promissory note, or a cheque, payable to bearer, and any person who takes the exchequer bill for value, and honestly, will acquire a perfectly good title, no matter what the title, or what the conduct, or what the authority, of the person with whom he is dealing. The moment, however, that the name is inserted in the exchequer bill, you take it from anyone other than the person whose name has been inserted at your peril, and if the person with whom you are dealing is not the true owner of the exchequer bill, but a man acting dishonestly, you will acquire no title, and you will lose your money, however honestly you may have acted. Therefore it is most important that a person in the City who is going to advance money on an exchequer bill should be aware that the moment that a name is inserted therein it ceases to be negotiable until the person whose name has been inserted indorses it, and that without his indorsement a person who takes an exchequer bill runs the risk of the transferor being the owner, or of his acting honestly. In *Brandao* v. *Barnett* it was held (and see the importance of it), that if the exchequer bills of A. be deposited by B. with a bank, the bank, not knowing that A. was the owner but believing that B. was the owner, the blanks in the exchequer bills not having been filled up, the bankers would acquire a lien upon the exchequer bills so deposited, and have a right to retain them as a security for any money due to them from him. They are deemed to be *bonâ fide* holders for value to the extent of their lien. In the case of *Brandao* v. *Barnett* the Court held that the circumstances of the deposit were such as to prevent the existence of a lien. If the exchequer bills are filled up with the name of the true owner, whatever the circumstances of the deposit, no lien otherwise than by the act of the true owner can exist. It is important for you to bear in mind these statements with respect to exchequer bills.

I come next to dividend warrants. Have you read *Partridge* v. *The Bank of England?* I dare say that you all have. It is found in the 9th Queen's Bench, the old Queen's Bench Reports, those venerable volumes.

that contain some of the earliest reporting work of
Lord Blackburn before he became a reporter under the
style of Ellis & Blackburn. I hope you will become
acquainted with the decisions reported in those
volumes also, in which are to be found some cases
admirably reported by the present Master of the
Rolls. No better training can be given to you than
to read and re-read some of these cases, first remark-
ing how the English lawyers, more closely than the
lawyers of any other country, can select the material
facts, which are alone necessary, for the determination of the question in dispute ; and then, secondly,
noticing the closeness of the reasoning in the decisions, which, even in present, and certainly in past
times, excites my admiration. Therefore, if you have
not done so, read the case of *Partridge* v. *The Bank
of England.* The dividend warrant in that case
was made payable to Mr. Partridge only. It was
in the following form : " To the Cashiers of the
Bank of England. Pay to Joseph Ashby Partridge
the sum of thirty-seven pounds ten shillings."
A person named Wakefield received the dividend
warrant under a power of attorney, and at the time he
received the warrant he wrote on the face of it an
acknowledgment of his having received of the Bank
of England the above-mentioned sum. Evidence was
given at the trial that after that acknowledgment
the cashiers at the Bank, according to long-established
custom, would pay the money to anybody who presented
the warrant. Wakefield passed the warrant to his
bankers, who took it *bonâ fide* and for value, and the
bankers passed it to the Bank of England. See the
error that was made ! Lord Denman and his colleagues
in the Queen's Bench, on proof that for sixty years the
dividend warrant so made out and receipted, had been
treated by the custom of merchants and bankers as a
negotiable instrument, decided in favour of the Bank
of England that the instrument, although not in its
nature and form a negotiable one, had become so by

the proof of usage. But look at the argument before the Judges in the Exchequer Chamber! How calmly and carefully every point is examined. They said: "It is of no use your bringing before us sixty years of usage. By the law of our country, an instrument made out in the way the instrument is in this case is not a negotiable instrument, and cannot be made so by the usage of merchants for sixty or any number of years," and they decided that the plaintiff was entitled to have the money as against the Bank of England. But of course a dividend warrant made out to Mr. Partridge, or order, would be a negotiable instrument, and I think, by virtue of the provisions of the 8th section, clause 4, of the Bills of Exchange Act, 1882, the instrument as drawn in the case of *Partridge* v. *The Bank of England* would now be deemed negotiable.

The negotiability of which I have been speaking is the creation of the common law, not of any statute. I can only find one case, and I shall be glad if you can help me to any other, in which it is said negotiability has been added by Act of Parliament as an incident to any document or instrument made on our own soil, and arising under our own law, and that is, the case of the bonds of the old East India Company. But I must confess that I want you to look at the Act of Parliament for yourselves. I question whether the words of the Act of Parliament, if taken strictly, really made them negotiable, or whether they did more than make them transferable. I told you on the last occasion that it is not because an instrument is transferable, so that the transferee can sue upon it in his own name, that it is negotiable. This principle must be added to the transferability, viz., that the instrument is one which a person taking *bonâ fide* and for value shall have a good title to, even although the person from whom he took it had none. If you look at *Glyn* v. *Baker*, in the 13th East, p. 509, and afterwards at the 51st George 3rd, chapter 64, section 4, you will find the section that is supposed to make the East India Bonds negotiable. Look at the section, and judge for yourselves whether it does so or not.

The doctrine which I have been, in a familiar way, trying to present to you, is, that if the instrument is one whose nature, incidents and effects are defined and regulated by English law, unless coming within the classes I have mentioned, it cannot be made negotiable by any usage, and only the legislature can make it so, since the Courts of law no longer affect to create or make law. To sum up: if a question arises as to the negotiability of an instrument created under our own law, you must call the attention of the Court to some statute, the express will of the legislature, making it so, or to some decision of our judges to which the legislature has given force and effect by enforcing their decision, and so impliedly making the principle involved in their decision the will of the legislature itself. So far, then, with respect to the negotiability of English instruments. I hope that I have not gone too rapidly for you, or spoken too hurriedly. I want you to realise this first part of my address, namely, what instruments are negotiable that are English instruments arising under English law, and I believe that I have enumerated the whole of them to you : viz. exchequer bills, bills of exchange, promissory notes, Bank notes, cheques, East India bonds and dividend warrants.

Now comes a very important part of our law with regard to foreign instruments, made by persons abroad, obligations arising under the law of foreign countries. The most important of these instruments relate to the public debts of foreign and colonial governments. I have told you that in certain events the law of England makes these negotiable by adopting the usage of our own markets. First of all you must learn this, that negotiability by usage applies to transactions taking place here, if you follow me. I have spoken to you of instruments arising under our law made in England. I am now going to speak to you of instruments not made here, but dealt in here. It is only so far as they are dealt in here that I am discussing the negotiability of the documents or instruments. Will you take this from me, that an instrument, however negotiable abroad, is not negotiable here, by the mere fact of its being negotiable abroad, and can only become negotiable here by the usage of our own markets. Even although the instrument might not be negotiable where it was made, yet if there was nothing on the face of it inconsistent with the right thereto passing to bearer by delivery, I think that our Courts would still apply the usage of our own market, if satisfied that, by a fairly continuous usage, the instrument passed by delivery, and that the person who took it honestly and for value acquired a title to the instrument itself. Do let me impress upon you that this is a most important part of our law, not to be trifled with or passed over lightly. I wish that our men of business in the City would turn some of their attention to this part of our law: When do foreign instruments become negotiable here by usage? It may be (I do not say that it is) that foreign instruments may by usage become negotiable here, although, perhaps, not negotiable abroad, if transferable by delivery abroad; and I will call your attention, step by step, to the way in which foreign instruments have been brought within the law relating to negotiable securities.

The first case that I know of in which a foreign instrument was treated as negotiable in this country is that of *Gorgier* v. *Mieville*, reported in the 3rd Barnewall & Cresswell, page 45. I look at the pages of that report with delight. The great decision upon which all the doctrine of the negotiability of foreign securities rests, a doctrine which has been discussed at such great length in so many pages during the last few years that even I weary in the examination—the arguments of counsel and the judgment of the Court are given in two pages! In that case the King of Prussia had by a bond declared himself and his successors bound to every person who should for the time being be the holder of the bond for the payment of the principal and interest. The plaintiff was the holder of the bond, and had deposited it with Agassiz & Co., who wrongfully pledged it with the defendants. Evidence was given that by the usage of the English market—not the usage of the Prussian market: nothing of the sort—that by the usage of the English market the property in an instrument such as I have described passed by delivery to every person who received it, and that the person who took it *bonâ fide* and for value acquired a title to it, just as if it were an exchequer bill. Did the judges hesitate to give effect to such usage? They could not have allowed such usage at all in the cases that I have been telling you about—English instruments. In such cases they were bound by English law and could not depart from it. But, dealing with a foreign instrument, they decided to adopt the usage of the merchants of their own country, and held not merely that the King of Prussia could discharge himself by paying the amount to bearer, but that the bond of the King of Prussia was, by the usage of the markets of England, a negotiable instrument, and consequently that any person who took it *bonâ fide* for value would acquire the property therein. The jury having found the defendants took the instrument *boná fide* and for an advance of money, the Court declared the defendants were entitled to the instrument to the extent of their advance. On that case has been built up all our law relating to the negotiability of foreign instruments dealt in on the English market. The case does not state how long the usage had lasted. It is clear the Court did not call for immemorial usage, as Kings of Prussia only came into existence in 1699, and the Court did not rely upon the plaintiff having any knowledge of such usage or of his acquiescing therein. Now, gentlemen, that case was recognized for nearly fifty years, and I have no doubt its doctrine was applied extensively in the English market and in the case of bonds of other countries. Its doctrine was not questioned until the case of *Goodwin* v. *Robarts* came up for consideration. The case of *Goodwin* v. *Robarts* is reported in L. R. 10 Exch. p. 76, where the decision of the Court of Exchequer will be found. In the same volume, p. 337, the decision of the Court of Appeal is reported; and the argument and the decision in the House of Lords will be found in Appeal Cases, vol. i. p. 476.

The plaintiff Goodwin had purchased £200 of Russian scrip, forming part of a loan raised by the Russian Government. The scrip was issued under the authority of the Russian Government. Messrs. Rothschild & Sons, of London, were employed to negotiate the loan. The form of the instrument was as follows:—Scrip for £100 stock, No.   . Received the sum of £20, being the first instalment of 20 per cent. upon £100 stock, and on payment of the remaining instalments at the periods specified, the bearer will be entitled to receive a definitive bond for £100, after receipt thereof, from the Imperial Government." Bonds were executed in Russia, and afterwards delivered to Messrs. Rothschild, who issued them in England and France to the bearers of the scrip. The bond declared, "The bearer of this bond is entitled to £100 sterling with interest at 5 per cent., which will be paid on presentation of the coupons hereunto attached." The plaintiff purchased his scrip through Clayton, his broker, and left the scrip with Clayton to be exchanged for bonds, or disposed of as he might direct. Clayton borrowed £800 for himself, and deposited as a security for the loan the scrip of the Russian loan belonging to the plaintiff.

In the special case presented to the Court for its opinion, it was admitted that the scrip of loans to foreign governments had been generally dealt in by bankers, money-dealers, and members of the English Stock Exchange, and through them by the public, for over fifty years, and the usage had been during all that time to buy and sell such scrip and advance loans of money upon the security of it before the bonds were issued, and to pass the scrip upon such dealing by mere delivery as negotiable instruments.

The question for the Court was, whether the defendants were entitled as against the plaintiff to the said scrip and to the proceeds thereof. The Court of Exchequer held that the defendants were so entitled; their decision was affirmed by the Court of Exchequer Chamber, and finally affirmed by the House of Lords. The House of Lords held there was no distinction to be made between the bonds themselves and the scrip that would entitle the person to the bonds, and the Law Lords recognized the authority of *Gorgier* v. *Mieville*, and gave effect to the principle of that case. The argument of Mr. Benjamin, who appeared for the appellant, but unsuccessfully, is worthy of a careful examination at your hands, because all the decisions relative to the matter are therein reviewed, and the objections to the defendants' claim most skilfully and powerfully urged. It is important to see how readily the Courts in these cases gave effect to the usage of the English market. The case of *Gorgier* v. *Mieville* was a recognition of the usage of merchants in making the bonds of a foreign government negotiable. In *Goodwin* v. *Robarts* the Courts proceeded a step further, and recognized the usage of merchants in making negotiable the scrip for foreign bonds; not the bonds themselves, but the scrip which promises that on certain payments being made a bond should be given. In reading the case of *Goodwin* v. *Robarts*, you must remember that the House of Lords placed the right of the defendants to the scrip on two grounds: first, on the ground that the scrip was a negotiable instrument, and had been taken by Robarts honestly and for value, and secondly on the ground that Goodwin was estopped by the form of the instrument from claiming it as against the defendant, because he was in the position of a person who had made a representation on the face of his scrip that it would pass with a good title to anyone on his taking it in good faith and for value, and who had put it in the power of his agent to hand over the scrip with this representation to those who were induced to alter their position on the faith of the representation so made.

Do not confound these two grounds together—they are entirely distinct, and the right on the ground of estoppel is in no way connected with the right arising out of the negotiability of the instrument. I may say for myself, that I never could follow the reasoning by which the peers based the claim of Robarts on the doctrine of estoppel, and I may mention that Lord Bramwell in a subsequent case dissented from the doctrine of *Goodwin* v. *Robarts,* so far as it rested on the doctrine of estoppel. Lord Bramwell (then Mr. Baron Bramwell) was one of the judges in the Court of Exchequer who gave judgment for the defendants, on the ground that they were entitled to judgment as being *bonâ fide* holders for value of a negotiable instrument.

You thus see that the doctrine of negotiability by usage was first applied to the bonds of foreign governments and then to the scrip for the bonds of foreign governments. I have now to call your attention to a still further advance in the application of this doctrine. I believe to-day, that the bonds of foreign companies, if negotiable by usage on the English market, would be regarded as such by our Courts. With respect to the bonds of foreign or colonial governments there is no contract upon which you can sue. You have a claim upon the governments but no cause of action. You cannot sue the Emperor of Russia here, and, so far as I know, not in his own empire. All you get by the purchase of Russian bonds is a piece of paper; nevertheless it is valuable paper; it is worth what it will fetch upon the market where men deal in Russian bonds. Thus the first steps ever taken in respect to making foreign instruments negotiable by usage were in cases in which apparently no contract subsisted between the parties by and to whom the bonds were delivered. To-day the doctrine has been applied to the bonds of foreign companies, which can contract and can incur responsibility, and whose engagements can be enforced against them by the law of the country under which they are put forth. You will find that it is decided that they may become negotiable here by usage. Remember always that in the case of foreign instruments which are negotiable by usage on the English market, the usage only applies to the acquisition of the property in the paper which evidences the transaction, and not in any way to the enforcement of the engagement itself. This will be seen on comparing *Goodwin* v. *Robarts* with *Crouch* v. *The Crédit Foncier Company*. In the former the question was who was entitled to the instruments: in the latter a person was attempting to sue upon a contract to which he was not originally a party. I have tried to go through all the cases and to find out what foreign instruments have been decided to be negotiable. In addition to those I have mentioned, in *Gorgier* v. *Mieville* and in *Goodwin* v. *Robarts*, you have Unified Egyptian bonds; Egyptian preference Government bonds; and New South Wales bonds. These last three kinds of foreign instruments were held to be negotiable in *The London & County Banking Company* v. *The London & River Plate Bank*, reported in Law Reports, 21 Queen's Bench Division, page 535. In that same case, reported in the Law Reports, Queen's Bench Division, vol. 20, page 232, it was decided that certificates of shares in the Pennsylvania Railway Company were not negotiable. And here I think is the distinction: if the foreign instrument which you claim to be negotiable here by usage shows on the face of it that a transferee is not to become the owner by mere delivery, but that something further is required in order to give him the property as in the case of the Pennsylvania Railway certificates of shares, which must be transferred in the books of the Company personally or by attorney, such instrument is not a negotiable security even by usage. It is important that men engaged in the City should know that Pennsylvania Railway certificates of shares are not negotiable instruments. They had been dealing in them and had regarded them as negotiable up to the time of the decision in 1887, but it has been decided that they are not, and such decision should be known. In the 15th Appeal Cases, page 268, in the case of *Cady* v. *London Chartered Bank of Australia*, it was held that certificates for shares in the New York Central Railway Company were not negotiable by usage. You will see this clearly stated in the judgment of Lord Herschell, page 285. It has been decided in *Easton* v. *The London Joint Stock Bank*, 34 Chancery Division, that Baltimore and Potomac Railway bonds are negotiable. If you look at the case you will find this peculiarity, that they, like the exchequer bills that I spoke of, pass by delivery until a name is inserted in the bond, and when a name is inserted they can only be transferred by entry in the books of the company. Therefore, as long as the Baltimore and Potomac Railway bonds have no name inserted in them they are negotiable securities. It was also decided that bonds of the Delaware and Hudson Railway Company were negotiable securities. In *Bentinck* v. *The London Joint Stock Bank*, Law Reports, 1893, 2 Chancery, p. 120, it was held that the bonds of the New York, Pennsylvania and Ohio Railway Company had become negotiable by usage. I think that, as far as I remember, those are the whole of the foreign securities which have been decided to be negotiable. With respect to foreign instruments, I think it must be taken that they cannot become negotiable by usage here, if it is necessary to do some act out of the kingdom in order to pass the title to them, or, in other words, if delivery is not of itself sufficient.

I should like to go a little further and tell you what instruments arising under English law are not negotiable. I have told you that certificates of shares, and scrip for certificates of shares in English companies—and I am going to make a statement now which may not be quite correct—that share warrants in English companies are not negotiable; but I think that if a foreign country should adopt share warrants, warrants that entitle the bearer to the shares specified in them, and they should be dealt in here, and by usage of our market they should be regarded as negotiable and pass irrevocably by delivery to a person who takes them *bonâ fide* and for value, as the validity of the transaction is to be determined by our own law, I believe that such warrants would be deemed by our Courts to be negotiable securities, unless the word securities is to be confined to instruments which provide for the payment of money. Lord Justice Bowen intimates that in his opinion share warrants arising under English law are not negotiable. On page 296 of Law Rep. Ch. 1891, vol. i., he says : " It is difficult to see how shares, share warrants, or certificates of shares in a company, which are not securities for money, can be entitled to the description of negotiable securities." I want you to read the statute of the 30th & 31st Victoria, chapter 131, sections 27 to 36, and those sections will give you all the provisions relating to the creation of share warrants. I have enquired and I have been told that they are not often resorted to in the case of companies existing under English law and carrying on business here. Section 27 provides that a company limited by shares, if authorized so to do by its regulations, may with respect to any share when it is fully paid up issue a warrant, stating that the bearer of the warrant is entitled to the share or shares. By section 28 it is prescribed that a share warrant shall entitle the bearer of such warrant to the shares specified in it, and that such shares may be transferred by the delivery of the share warrant. There are no words which say that anybody who takes a share warrant *bonâ fide* and for value shall become entitled to it. I think that it is sufficient to put this construction upon the sections, that they provide that the lawful bearer of the share warrant shall be entitled to the shares. But you must look at the case of *Little* v. *The Joint Stock Banking Company*, reported in the same volume as *Simmons' Case* and argued together with it. Little claimed seventy-five shares of £10 each in the Rio Tinto Company, Limited. That was an English company, and as regards those shares, share warrants had been issued under the Companies Act, 1867, section 27. The Joint Stock Bank by their counsel claimed those shares as being negotiable. As the Court of Appeal was ready to decide against the Bank, assuming the share warrants to be negotiable, the question of their negotiability was allowed to pass without much discussion, Lord Justice Bowen, as above stated, intimating that in his opinion they were not negotiable. I think it must be taken at present that share warrants in English companies are not negotiable and cannot be made so by usage.

So far, then, to-night. I have one or two observations to make to you upon a matter which I must mention before I sit down. I will sum up this evening's lecture at the introduction of the next lecture. I have made every endeavour to give you to the best of my ability a list of all the instruments that at present have been decided to be negotiable. With respect to those arising under our own law I have relied upon Mr. Justice Blackburn's judgment in *Crouch* v. *The Crédit Foncier*. Take that away and then I have no justification for the distinction which I have drawn; but if you follow that decision you have clear and direct guidance with respect to instruments arising under English Law. If you adopt the view that share warrants under the Act of 1867, chapter 131, are negotiable instruments, then you must add them to the list, and may you soon in your profession be called upon to discuss the question whether they are, and aid the Court to a just determination. I have given you a list of foreign securities, and I cannot impress upon you sufficiently the necessity of separating the instruments which arise under our own law, and those which are created in foreign countries by foreign Governments and foreign companies.

Then, let me say that in using the phrase "negotiable instruments," I should like to use that phrase as included under the wider term of negotiable property so that negotiable property should include negotiable chattels and negotiable instruments. I have only found the words "negotiable property" used once by a Judge. I wish to tell you that there are negotiable chattels as well as negotiable instruments. No interest in land can be negotiable. The Chancery Judges have not yet established negotiable interests in land, and therefore you may get rid of land. And I also tell you that there are no negotiable chattels except of a particular kind, to wit, the current coin of the realm and the pieces of paper on which the negotiable instruments are written. By legislation a title to chattels under certain circumstances may be acquired when dealing with persons who have no property therein or authority to deal with them, but chattels have not yet been made negotiable. Do not speak of chattels dealt with under the Acts of the Legislature as having "some of the elements of negotiability." If you have two material objects you can say that they have two or more elements in common, but where you speak of intellectual conceptions, you cannot safely do so. Keep them distinct and use distinct names. If they are alike you use the same word; if not, have a distinct word. Never use the words " elements of negotiability " in respect of personal chattels. True, we have by legislation now given rights to persons who purchase chattels or advance money on them far beyond what existed even when I came to the Bar. A mercantile agent entrusted with goods may by sale and disposition of them defraud the true owner, and give a good title to the man who buys. If you buy seventeen volumes of Meeson and Welsby, and pay for them, the property in the books vests in you; but if you leave them in the shop, and the shopkeeper sells them to someone else *bonâ fide* and for value, by the provisions of recent legislation you lose your property in the books. We also know, too, that if you agree to sell a man goods who is to pay for them by instalments and you put him in possession of the goods before he has paid the instalments, and he sells them, the man who purchases them *bonâ fide* will have a good title, although it was stipulated that the property in the goods should not pass until all the instalments had been paid. But there is no statute and no rule of common law which says that personal chattels under all circumstances, at all times and in all places, shall pass to the person who buys them *bonâ fide* and for value. You must enquire into the nature and extent of the authority that has been conferred by Acts of Parliament in respect of the disposition of chattels, and particularly study the Factors Act of the year 1889. But the negotiability of the instruments with which I am dealing is limited to no time, no place, no person. Wherever or from whomsoever a man takes them, if he takes them *bonâ fide* and for value, he will acquire a perfectly good title; and although Dr. Johnson was allowed to write by permission in Goldsmith's *Deserted Village—*

"Trade's proud empire hastes to swift decay,"

we are still extending our commerce year by year, and the principles of law to which I have called your attention to-night have materially assisted in such development and expansion. I thank you for your kind and patient hearing.

NEGOTIABLE PROPERTY.

Negotiable Instruments.

Instruments existing under English Law.
Bills of Exchange.
Promissory Notes.
Bank Notes.
Cheques.
Exchequer Bills.
East India Bonds.
Dividend Warrants.
Share Warrants.
Little v. London Joint Stock Bank.
Quaere—see Lord Justice Bowen's statement in *Simmons v. London Joint Stock Bank*, 1 Chan. App. 1891, p. 296.

By Evidence of Usage of English Markets.
Bonds of Foreign and Colonial Governments; Bonds of Foreign Companies.
Gorgier v. Mieville.
Bonds of King of Prussia.
Goodwin v. Robarts.
Scrip of Russian Government for Bonds payable to bearer; Austro-Hungarian Scrip.
London & County Bank v. London & River Plate Bank.
Unified Egyptian Bonds.
Egyptian Preference Bonds.
New South Wales Bonds.
Simmons v. London Joint Stock Bank.
Cedulas or Bonds of the Buenos Ayres Land Mortgage Bank.
Easton v. London Joint Stock Bank.
Baltimore and Potomac Railway Bonds.
Delaware and Hudson Railway Bonds.
Bentinck v. London Joint Stock Bank.
Bonds of New York, Pennsylvania and Ohio Railroad Company.

Not negotiable.
Pennsylvania Railway Certificate of Shares.
Certificate for Shares in the New York Central Railway Company.

Negotiable Chattels.
Current Coin of the Realm.
The Paper on which Negotiable Instruments have been written.

LECTURE III.

On the last occasion when I had the honour of speaking to you, I endeavoured to present to you a full list of all the negotiable instruments which have been declared to be such by the decisions of our Courts, and I particularly called your attention to one decision, and perhaps the most important of all, viz., the case of *Crouch* v. *The Crédit Foncier Company*, which, if the judgment of Lord Blackburn stands, leads you to this conclusion—that no usage on the Stock Exchange or elsewhere can make an instrument that is created in this country and defined and regulated by English law negotiable; and that whether an instrument created under English law is negotiable or not, is a question of law to be determined by the Judge before whom the question arises. If that decision be correct, then I showed you that with respect to instruments arising under English law the principal and perhaps the only instruments that could be deemed to be negotiable were when they were in a certain condition, bills of exchange, promissory notes, bank notes, cheques, exchequer bills, East India bonds and dividend warrants. I then called your attention to the case of foreign instruments, thus dividing the subject of negotiable instruments into two classes: one, instruments arising under our own law, and made here in England; and the other, instruments created abroad and arising under foreign law; and I endeavoured to show you by the decisions to which I called your attention that if foreign instruments become negotiable here by usage, that is if the property indicated by them passes by simple delivery, and if persons taking them *bonâ fide* and. for value acquire a good title, then the Courts of this country would declare them to be negotiable in any proceeding here, and would upon the evidence of such usage annex the incident of negotiability to nearly all instruments created by foreign or colonial Governments who are borrowing and creating a debt, and to the bonds and engagements of foreign companies.

I called your attention to the decision in the House of Lords in *Simmons' case*, which applied the doctrine of negotiability by usage not merely to the bonds of a foreign Government, in which case there is perhaps no contract subsisting at all upon which the person who holds the bond can sue, but to the case of bonds of foreign companies who might be sued by the holder of the bonds in the country in which those bonds were given. I also endeavoured to shew by a reference to two cases to which I called your attention that if the instruments on the face of them indicate that something is to be done in the foreign country in order that the property in them should pass, that then, in that case, whatever may be the usage of English bankers and brokers, such instruments are not negotiable.

Then I called your attention to the statement of law that instruments which are negotiable abroad are not thereby negotiable here, and that you would require evidence of usage in this country to give negotiability to such instruments. Then I passed on to tell you that with respect to personal chattels, they are not negotiable with but two exceptions, and that those exceptions were the chattels which constitute the current coin of the realm and the paper that evidences the negotiable instruments. The law of this country apparently is clear that, with the exception of a few instances, no person who takes a personal chattel can acquire a better title than the person who transferred it could confer, and that the person who is the owner of a personal chattel, as I am of my books in my chambers, remains the owner of that chattel as I remain the owner of my books; and if, to-night, any person were to break into my chambers and steal my books, except by sale in market overt, he could not confer any title to them. Mr. Justice Willes in a judgment in *Fuentes* v. *Montes*, reported in Law Reports, 3 Common Pleas, discusses the whole question under what circumstances a man can at Common Law acquire a better title to chattels than the person with whom he deals is capable of conferring. He gives three instances: (1) sale in market overt; (2) the case of a man who has acquired the property in goods, under a contract obtained by fraud, and who has resold such goods to a *bonâ fide* purchaser for value before the defrauded vendor has rescinded the contract; and thirdly, the case of a holder of a bill of lading parting with the instrument for value to a *bonâ fide* purchaser, whilst the goods were *in transitu*, and that such a disposition would deprive the vendor of his right of stoppage *in transitu*, in case of the insolvency of the vendee.

Then I called your attention to one or two instances of instruments said to be negotiable which are not. You will find in one or two arguments of counsel, and in an occasional judgment, it is stated, without any qualification, that a bill of lading is a negotiable instrument. It is not, and if you will look into the case of *Gurney* v. *Behrend*, reported in 3 Ellis & Blackburn, 622, you will find it distinctly laid down that a bill of lading is not a negotiable instrument. More than that, in a recent important judgment in the House of Lords, *Sewell* v. *Burdick*, L. R. 10 App. Cases, 74, there is this difference indicated between a bill of exchange and a bill of lading, viz., that the effect of what passes and arises in dealing with a bill of lading, depends upon the intention of the parties; and upon the existence of a transaction fitted to pass the property apart from the delivery of the bill of lading, and consequently that a transfer of a bill of lading will pass the entire property, or a portion only of that property according to the intention of the parties. Then, of course, in the case of a bill of lading, if a man simply indorses it to his factor or agent, no property passes; but if I have a bill of exchange, of which I am the true owner for value, I can, without any consideration, pass the property in it at once to any person I choose. Moreover, until the 18 & 19 Vict. c. 111, no one could sue upon the contract contained in the bill of lading unless he was originally a party to such contract.

I want you, however, to bear in mind, that the current coin of the realm, such as sovereigns, half-crowns, and shillings, all pass to the person who takes them *bonâ fide* for value, irrespective altogether of the title of the person who transfers them; and you thus have an instance of chattels, the property in which may be derived not from the true owner, or anything that he has done, but from the conduct of the person who receives them. I have to impress upon you that the true view of negotiability is this: that a person can claim the property in negotiable instruments or the current coin of the realm by what he has done—not by what anybody else has done; and that having taken sovereigns or Bank of England notes for value, and honestly, he is entitled to retain them, no matter who the party is who deals with him, or what the circumstances of the transaction.

Now, if you want to see the law relating to the transfer of the current coins of the realm and bank notes, I refer you to the case of *Miller* v. *Race*, 1 Sm. L. C. 491, 9th ed., which I hope you will all read. Do not let it be said that the reason why property in money passes to the *bonâ fide* holder for value is because you cannot follow or trace it. Nothing of the kind. You can follow money; and if you can trace it and identify it, you can sue for its value and recover it from any person who cannot justify its detention. On the other hand, if you mark all the current coins and bank notes in your possession, so that you could speak with certainty to every one, you may yet without any fault or act of your own, lose the whole, although you know in whose possession they are. Suppose a burglar steals them all and they have come into the possession of a tradesman who has taken them *bonâ fide* and for value, you cannot demand them from him, notwithstanding your power of shewing they once were yours, and that you had never parted with them. The tradesman has become the owner of them by the principle of law to which I have so constantly referred you. So far, therefore, understand me, I do not know of any personal chattels which are negotiable other than the current coins of the realm and the paper on which negotiable instruments are written. I am quite aware of cases in which, perhaps, a better title may be had than the person transferring could give, and of course I am not insensible to the cases in equity where a purchaser of the legal estate, without notice, may get a better title, or to the case of the assignment of a chose in action, where a creditor has dealt twice with the debt due to him, the second assignee, who should give notice of the assignment to the debtor (the first not having done so), would acquire the right to the debt. I am not insensible to those cases, and I hope you will put down a list of them, and all learn, as you ought to do, if you are to be competent for your work, when, and under what circumstances, a person can acquire a title which the man with whom he was dealing could not himself lawfully confer.

Having said thus much, let me tell you that with respect to the bonds of foreign Governments, the scrip for bonds of foreign Governments, the bonds of foreign companies, the scrip for bonds of foreign companies, I have told you nearly all the law relating to them. I have to tell you that with respect to them there is no drawer, no acceptor, no indorser, no notice of dishonour needful, and none of those duties to be discharged which exist in respect of bills of exchange. The main thing in connexion with foreign instruments is to know whether they are negotiable, whether the property in them has been lawfully passed, and, if not, whether the claimant has taken them *bonâ fide* and for value. I now advance to consider those negotiable instruments which do involve a great deal of learning in order to their proper use and enjoyment, namely bills of exchange, promissory notes, and cheques.

Now, before proceeding to discuss them, if there should be any here to-night who are engaged in the City, I should like to address to them, with your permission, a word or two of advice. You who are lawyers have had quite enough law already in these lectures to occupy your spare hours for some time to come. To those persons here who are unaccustomed to the consideration of legal decisions, they perhaps may be glad to listen to a few general observations that do not come under the head of law. The observations which I now offer are such as were addressed to myself in my early years.

Now I should like to impress on you young men in the City (whether acting for a master or on your own account), the importance of endeavouring to procure in every transaction in business or trade the promise that a bill of exchange shall be given. To secure such promise, you see frequently on the invoices in the City the proviso, "Cash at the end of the month, less $2\frac{1}{2}$ per cent., or a three months' bill." There is nothing more important in trade than having such an agreement as that. Without such agreement you cannot call upon your customer to give you his acceptance. You can have such an agreement by express arrangement with the buyer, or it may arise from previous dealings. If having promised to accept he does not do so, you can sue him at once for breach of his agreement, and obtain in the action the full price of the goods less the discount. The bill of exchange, if you can get it, is a thing that is readily convertible in the money market of London. If you cannot get cash, get as many of your transactions as you can back again in your cash box in the form of bills of exchange. You may find yourself pressed for money through failure of people to keep their engagements, or an opportunity may offer of making a good purchase for cash. It is no use a man taking his book debts to discount houses or bankers for an advance—they will not look at them; but if you have bills you can walk into a bill-broker's office (as it has been my business to do), and offer good trade bills with names well known in the various towns in the kingdom, and in a moment you can turn them into money. I have known a man relieved from most pressing engagements because he could go and get a considerable sum of money by discounting bills of exchange which he had taken in respect of trade transactions. Another thing to remember is this— that if once people have put their hands to bills as acceptors they will do their utmost to meet them, because of the fatal consequence of their dishonour; whereas a debt that is merely in the books of the creditor may be long delayed; and the creditor does not care to sue a man who, though slow in payment, is yet faithful. These bills of exchange are not things to be trifled with. The moment you put your hand to a bill of exchange it goes away—it circulates everywhere. Let me give a further piece of advice. Pray mind, you young men, to keep a proper list of the bills which your master accepts, and do not allow him to accept a bill until it has been put into the "Bills payable" book, so that there may be no mistake as to his obligations. I cannot stay to tell you to-night of the troubles which I myself have known through forgetfulness so to do. Another thing is, take care to keep your bills in proper order and nice condition. Do not take to a bill-broker a parcel of bills which may never have been in anybody else's hands but which are in such a state that they look as if they had been hawked about for discount to other houses. Keep your bills in proper order, that they really look like good trade bills that you are presenting to the bill discounter. There is another thing I should wish you to remember. Do not, you young men, be parties to creating bills of exchange behind which there is no value, or creating what is called accommodation paper. This is sometimes done, to the discredit of men engaged in business. If you are an honest man and of sound position, and the man who desires to assist you to raise money is honest too, go and tell your banker how you stand and what you desire to do, and unless I am mistaken he will do all he can to render you assistance; but bankers do not like to deal with a man who has presented to them apparently honest trade bills, and all the while they are unconnected with any trade transaction. Honesty is the best policy.

Now, having uttered these few words, that are not quite in the line of my lectures, let me, with your permission, just call your attention to one or two cases which show the risks you run in creating bills of exchange. For this purpose I must ask you to read the case of *Ingham* v. *Primrose*, which is reported in 7 Common Bench, New Series, page 82. This is a case which shows how careful you should be when dealing with bills. If ever you have put your name to a bill of exchange as acceptor, and still more, if it has got a drawer's name to it, and you do not wish to make any use of it, do not tear it in pieces, mind that you burn it or completely cancel or deface it. In the case of *Ingham* v. *Primrose* the defendant, being desirous of raising some money, had accepted a bill, drawn by one Charles Murgatroyd and given it to him for the purpose of getting it discounted. Murgatroyd tried to get the bill discounted, but in vain, and returned the bill to the defendant, who said: "I will tear it up; it is of no use. We cannot do the bill;" and he tore the paper in half and threw it away in the street. Charles Murgatroyd picked the bill up and afterwards pasted the two pieces together and passed the bill away to a man named King, from whom the plaintiff took it. At the trial it was found as a fact that the defendant when he tore the bill in half and threw it away intended to cancel it. The jury having found that King took the bill *bonâ fide* and for value, the Court held that Primrose, the acceptor, was liable. I am bound to tell you that the present Master of the Rolls, in the case of *Baxendale* v. *Bennett*, which is reported in Law Reports, 3 Queen's Bench Division, page 525, has cast some doubt on the propriety of that decision. The case which called for the observations of Lord Esher did not require perhaps the consideration of the case of *Ingham* v. *Primrose*, because in *Ingham* v. *Primrose* the defendant had accepted the bill with a drawer's name upon it. He knew that Charles Murgatroyd picked up the torn pieces, and the defendant left them in Murgatroyd's hands. But there is the case of *Baxendale* v. *Bennett*, which you will look at in conjunction with *Ingham* v. *Primrose*. In the case of *Ingham* v. *Primrose* it may be said that the instrument had ceased to exist, and was never after issued as such by the acceptor, and therefore there was no instrument which could be passed to a *bonâ fide* holder for value. The Court, however, repelled the objection and thought that the acceptor was liable because the cancellation was not sufficiently complete. In the case of *Baxendale* v. *Bennett* the defendant had written his name as acceptor across a bill stamp. There was no drawer's name upon it. It was stolen from his desk, and a drawer's name was put upon it without the authority of the acceptor. Such drawing need not necessarily have been a forgery because, as Lord Justice Bramwell pointed out, the man who stole the paper might have said to the person who took it: "I have the authority of the acceptor to put any name I like, and you can put your own name as drawer;" and the person who took it may have put his name as a drawer quite honestly. It was held in that case that the *bonâ fide* holder for value could not recover, because the defendant had never accepted a bill of exchange—he had never authorised anyone to put his name to the instrument as drawer, and without a drawer's name, authorised expressly or impliedly, there cannot be a bill of exchange. The grounds on which *Baxendale* v. *Bennett* was decided do not, in my opinion, involve the reversal of *Ingham* v. *Primrose*. *Baxendale* v. *Bennett*, however, shews that a man may give full value for an instrument that appears to be in order and every signature to which is genuine and has been honestly placed there, and yet the *bonâ fide* holder have no remedy against the supposed acceptor.

Now I have called your attention to the consequence of not getting the instrument properly endorsed, as was shown in the case of *Whistler* v. *Forster*, which I have mentioned to you two or three times. The plaintiff there took the cheque *bonâ fide* and for value, but did not notice that the payee had not endorsed it. He got no title by mercantile law and usage, and before he could get the endorsement he had notice that the payee had committed a fraud in procuring the cheque. Held, that he could not have a better title to the cheque than the person who passed it to him, and as such person had obtained it by fraud the person who gave value for the bill had no title either.

Now let me call the attention of men of business to another case, which shows the importance of using the utmost care in dealing with bills. In the case of *Garrard* v. *Lewis*, which is reported in 10 Q. B. D., p. 30, a person accepted a bill, which, by some oversight, did not contain words in the body of the bill which expressed the amount for which the bill was drawn, a place having been left in the body of the bill for such words. The amount expressed by figures in the margin was £14 0s. 6d. The drawer of the bill wrote in the body of the bill in words *one hundred and sixty-four pounds and sixpence*, and altered the marginal figures from £14 0s. 6d. to £164 0s. 6d. A person took the bill so altered *bonâ fide* and for value: Held, that he had a perfectly good title—that the marginal figures are not an essential part of the bill;

that the words are the essential part of the bill in determining the amount; and that the alteration of the figures was not a material alteration so as to avoid the instrument. In that case the acceptor had to pay the £164 0s. 6d., although he only intended to pay £14 0s. 6d. I have just given you those three or four instances, and now let me give you another, because I think you will learn more about bills of exchange in this way, as I shall shew you directly, than from the longest and most accurate definition that ever was prepared. A tradesman was to have the acceptance of A. B. for goods sold and delivered to him, and C. D. was to be surety for their payment. A bill was drawn upon A. B. only. A. B. accepted it, and then it was said, "Well, now, Mr. Surety, you had better accept," and so he did. Held, no acceptance. Why? Because a man cannot accept a bill unless it is addressed to him. To be an acceptor he must be a drawee. Here the only drawee was A. B., and A. B. was the only person who could accept. The bill should have been drawn on C. D. as well as A. B. There being no debt between C. D. and the tradesman, and C. D. not being liable on the bill as an acceptor, the tradesman would have no claim against C. D., unless the instrument itself to which he put his name as acceptor would satisfy the provisions of the fourth section of the Statute of Frauds (see *Jackson v. Hudson*, 2 Campbell, 447). If you are going to have an acceptor see that he is a drawee. I just call your attention to these few things really to awaken in you a great interest in this department of our law, whether you practise the profession of the law or whether you are engaged in commercial houses. To my mind, men should study this portion of our law until they are practically masters of its rules, principles, and decisions; and to men of business and bankers it is of the utmost importance that they should know these things in order that they may prove themselves exact in everything they do, and especially if they are servants, because there is not a more delightful work than that of a servant guarding by his care and competency the interests of the master whom he serves.

I come now to bills of exchange themselves, and I am bound to tell you that the law relating to them has been codified by an Act of Parliament called the 45th and 46th Victoria, cap. 61. It contains 100 sections. This Act will, I think, be a dead letter to you if you begin to read it through without some such preparation as that which I am endeavouring to give you. It is indeed a valley of dry bones, and an informing spirit is needful that they may live.

It is not easy for the experienced lawyer to master all its contents; and although I have read it through several times, and have had some experience in the application of its provisions, if you were to examine me as to some portions of it you might not think me so well acquainted with the law of bills of exchange as I may appear to you to be.

Now do not let us begin with a *definition* of a bill. Definition may be all very well in examinations; yet I have known men in attempting to give definitions omit a word here and a word there that evidently told me that the individual giving the definition was a respectable person carrying a burden the nature of which he did not quite appreciate or understand.

Now let us look at the enormous definition of a bill of exchange given in the Act of 1882. Just imagine keeping this in your mind, "A bill of exchange is an unconditional order in writing, addressed by one person to another, signed by the person giving it, requiring the person to whom it is addressed to pay on demand or at a fixed or determinable future time, a sum certain in money to or to the order of a specified person, or to bearer."

I trust that before we have finished this course of Lectures I shall by practical instances set up the whole of this definition in your minds piece by piece, and cause it to remain there without the effort of memory: that you may have it as a living thing in your minds and not as mere words repeated by rote.

I think, I hope so at least, that I shall render you more service, by putting before you specimens of the instruments themselves which have given rise to discussions in our courts, than by examining in a scholastic manner the various parts of the definition I have just read to you. On the next occasion I hope to put in your hands a set of papers which will enable me to speak more freely and easily to you on the subject of drawer, drawee, payee, acceptor, indorsee, and other matters. But to-night I want, if you will allow me, to get into your minds portions of the definition of a bill of exchange by shewing you some of the transactions, that are valid at common law, which cannot be carried out by a bill of exchange, and some transactions that can be carried out by bills of exchange, which cannot be carried out by the ordinary rules of the common law or equity, and some incidents to bills of exchange which do not attach to contracts at common law. Some people to whom I have talked have looked upon a bill of exchange as something mysterious; and I remember (when I was attending the lectures of Mr. Broom), a fellow-student saying to me, "Well, I have never seen a bill of exchange myself, and although I have taken down a number of phrases from this good lecturer, the whole thing is still to me a mystery."

Now, I think we shall do well to look first at a bill of exchange in the way I am putting it to you. First of all, take this. There are great privileges incident to bills of exchange, as you will see directly: there are therefore necessary limitations, and there are many transactions that can be carried through at common law that cannot be comprised in, or covered by, a bill of exchange.

Now, first of all, I must shew you under what head of contracts a bill of exchange is found, and I only hope that everybody will be able to follow me. I may be right or wrong about it, but if ever I am asked what a *contract* is, I always say it is "an agreement to which the supreme power has annexed an obligation." In the language of Austin and of Maine it is an agreement plus an obligation. I never use the word "agreement" as synonymous with "contract." Then you see I have to look and ascertain, first of all, whether there is an agreement of parties. If there be, then the next thing to ascertain is: Are all the conditions there which must be present in order that the agreement may have a binding force or effect? This question I answer by having ascertained by examination of statutes and the decisions of judges to what agreements the supreme power has decided to give a binding force or annex an obligation. Thus the study of the law of contracts involves the same kind of investigation as that of the man of science who arranges flowers or animals in different classes.

Now, by the law of England, you may take it that, apart from judgments and contracts of Record, contracts are divided into two great classes—contracts under seal and simple contracts. A bill of exchange comes under the head of simple contracts, and if an instrument is under seal it is not a bill of exchange at all, unless the drawing of a bill of exchange under seal is authorised by statute. Lord Blackburn has said there is no case in the books where a bill of exchange made under seal has been sued on. You know, in order that there may be an agreement obligatory under the head of "Simple Contracts," you must find in the transaction somewhere or other a request, a consideration, and a promise, all combining with the intention of entering into a binding engagement. Now the bill of exchange is an excellent illustration of this rule, because it introduces you at once to the request made by the drawer, the promise made by the acceptor, and the consideration which must always be present for a bill.

Now I want to call attention to a peculiarity with respect to the consideration for a bill of exchange. If there be a consideration for it, it does not matter from whom it moves. In a simple contract the only person who can sue upon it is the person from whom the consideration moves. Take the case of *Tweedle* v. *Atkinson*, which is reported in 1 Best & Smith, p. 393. The plaintiff there was engaged to a young lady, and her father promised him verbally that he would give him a marriage portion. The marriage took place without the promise being performed. Subsequently the father of the plaintiff and the father of the young lady met, and the latter said to the former: "I will give £200 to your son if you will also give him £100." The father of the young man said he was content to do so, and the proposal was accepted. The son cannot sue either his own father or his father-in-law for the payment of either of the sums. Although his advancement was the object of the contract, he was not a party to the transaction. The consideration did not move from him. The consideration was not marriage; the consideration was the promise to give £200 if the other would give £100. Although all that passed between the parents was by word of mouth, there is no question of the Statute of Frauds. The marriage was not the consideration, and the only person who could sue is the one father suing the other for the non-fulfilment of the promise. But now, then, let one father put down the cash and hand it to the son. Let the other father give a promissory note for £200 to his son-in-law. Then the son-in-law can sue on the promissory note if dishonoured, although the consideration for the note did not move from him. He has got the promissory note with a consideration for it; and in the case of a promissory note or bill of exchange it does not matter from whom the consideration moves if there be an actual consideration for the note or bill.

Observe another thing with respect to the consideration for a bill of exchange. There is always a presumption that a bill of exchange or promissory note has been given for a consideration. It is not a conclusive presumption. Evidence may be given to shew that there was in fact no consideration for the bill. There is no such presumption in the case of other contracts coming under the head of simple contracts. As between acceptor and drawer, indorser and indorsee, the presumption is that a consideration has been given.

Now take the next point of importance to work out this definition. A promissory note or a bill of exchange to exist must relate to debt and debt only; so also it must be debt in the strictest sense of the word; not debt and some other obligation and promise, but debt and debt only. I do not know whether you ever read any good pleadings—I do not often see any now,—but if you look to the money counts in Bullen and Leake, you will find that when suing for money payable under the money counts you could always recover as a debt the value of anything you had supplied, although no price was fixed by the bargain, the law implying in such case that a reasonable price is to be paid. That was still regarded as a transaction in debt, and for which an action of debt would lie. "Please pay the reasonable price due for the goods I sold you," will not do for a bill of exchange; it must be a fixed or certain sum for which you draw. If you drew an instrument thus: "Please pay me the balance you owe me in respect of cottages erected," it would not be a bill of exchange. In all these cases, claims would arise at common law, but not one could be the subject of a bill of exchange. Again, in order that the instrument should be a bill of exchange, the request must not be conditional. Suppose you were to draw upon me for the money due and owing in respect of the proceeds of goods I sold for you, that would not be good as a bill of exchange. Suppose you requested me to pay a sum of money on the arrival of a certain ship, upon the sale of a certain cargo, or the delivery of certain bills of lading, even if accepted, the instrument would not be a bill of exchange. The request must be pure and simple, and free from all condition. Every one of the transactions I have just named might give rise to a claim at common law, yet cannot be made the subject-matter of a bill of exchange. If the instrument is drawn conditionally on the happening of a certain event, it is none the less invalid as a bill of exchange, even although the event happened before the time mentioned on the instrument for the performance of the obligation had expired.

Again, let me take another illustration. Bills of exchange and promissory notes have this advantage over transactions at common law, that they fix the time for payment beyond all dispute. You need not trouble yourself to consider whether the day mentioned on the bill was the day originally agreed on for payment by the original contract, or whether there was any consideration for the promise to pay on a fixed day. If your debtor has given you a bill of exchange, such bill constitutes conditional payment. You cannot sue him for the original debt while the bill is running, and when the day comes he must pay it, whether the time of the bill was fixed by the original contract or not.

Now I will give this illustration to you young gentlemen. Suppose you went into a tailor's shop, and he said: "You owe me £15 for clothes." "Yes, sir, I am sorry I do; well, I will pay you on the first of next month, because then I get my allowance." You could not be sued upon that promise. There is no consideration for it. I do not mean to say that a judge would not amend if the creditor did happen to declare upon such promise, but such promise has no force or effect whatever. If you want to see an instance of this in the old days, look at *Hopkins* v. *Logan*, which is reported in 5 Meeson and Welsby, page 241, where the declaration alleged that the plaintiff and defendant had stated an account whereby certain sums of money were due and owing to the plaintiff, and the defendant promised to pay the said moneys on a certain day to come; that the said day had passed before bringing the action, and the defendant had not paid the money. The Court held that the declaration disclosed no cause of action, because it did not allege any consideration for the promise; the promise which arises upon an account stated is to pay on request, and a promise to pay on a fixed day would not be binding without some fresh consideration; and as in those days there was no amendment, the proceedings were of no avail, although the defendant owed every penny of the money claimed. The moral is, get a bill of exchange for your debt whenever you can.

There is another thing which I will just point out. At common law, if for a consideration you promise to pay on a particular day, on that day you must tender the money to the creditor. It is not so with a bill of exchange, because if a bill of exchange is not payable on demand, you have always three days of grace for the payment; hence, if the bill is drawn on the 1st March, and is payable in three months, then it would be payable on the 4th June.

If you keep these things in your minds you will soon come with pleasure and delight to the definition in the Act of Parliament, and see it all for yourselves, and be able to speak of it in your own way. Of course, you know that in Courts of law you are seldom asked for a definition of a bill of exchange. You produce the instrument; objection is taken to it, and you must answer the objection that is presented. Another thing in respect of which a bill of exchange differs from a simple contract debt is this: a bill of exchange gives rise to a claim for interest unless there is a stipulation to the contrary. On a bill of exchange, I may say at once, that if the instrument contains nothing to the contrary, interest is payable, and usually at five per cent., from the day of its maturity, whereas interest is not payable upon debts at common law apart from agreement, express or implied. You may now, however, recover interest on debts as damages if they come within the terms of the Act of 3 & 4 Will. IV., c. 42, sec. 27.

Now I want to tell you of transactions which a bill of exchange can carry out which are carried out at common law, but are carried out by bills of exchange with additional powers and facilities. A creditor may in writing request his debtor to pay the debt he owes to a third person, and the creditor may give such request to the third person. Such an instrument is an authority to pay. If the debtor pays, he has discharged his debt, and the receipt of the money by the third person may discharge a debt due to him from the person giving the authority or constitute the person giving the authority the creditor of the person receiving it. A bill of exchange may carry out such authority by being drawn in favour of a third person. Such third person is called the payee, and answers to the person at common law to whom the authority to receive is given. But there is this difference between an order to pay at common law and a bill of exchange. The man who receives an authority at common law cannot sue the debtor for the amount due, the relation of debtor and creditor does not subsist between them, nor can he sue as being assignee of the debt; but, as I have told you that so long as there is a consideration for the bill anyone may sue although the consideration does not move from him, the payee of a bill of exchange can demand the sum due on the bill from the acceptor and sue him if he does not pay. The man who has a mere common law authority cannot sue the debtor if he does not pay: all he can do is to go back to his own debtor and say, "I am very sorry to tell you that your creditor has not paid; you must now pay me." Look at the decision in *Percival* v. *Dunn*, which is reported in 29 Chancery Division, page 128, a decision of Vice-Chancellor Bacon. He held in that case, that a document drawn in the following words, "Please pay Percival the amount of his account £42 14s. 6d. for goods supplied," was not an instrument upon which any action would lie at the suit of Percival; it was a simple request to pay, and no action would lie. It did not amount to an assignment, and therefore no action upon the instrument delivered by the creditor to Percival could be maintained.

Now I want particularly, in the few minutes that remain at my disposal to-night, to call your attention to the most important part of the transactions that are carried out by bills of exchange, viz., the assignment of debt. Bills of exchange have rendered debt a marketable commodity capable of being assigned in the easiest and simplest manner. Now from what I have to tell you presently you will see that the things I have mentioned hitherto all arise on the face of the instrument. You find the acceptance on the face as a rule—it need not be there, but you generally find it there. You will find the name of the drawee there; you will find the name of the drawer there, and the name of the payee there, the amount, the dates, the time; all will appear on the face of the instrument; and when we go quietly through the form of a bill of exchange I shall ask you to make yourselves familiar with all that is on the face of it before ever you turn your attention to what will be on the back of it. The back of the bill itself ordinarily relates to the assignment of the debt mentioned on the face, and except, of course, the drawing in favour of the payee, which may be regarded as an exception, I still like to say that the *back* of the bill contains all that relates to the assignment of the debt, and on the back of the instrument will be found the transactions containing the names and signatures by which the debt is assigned.

Now, you can do a very great deal at common law and equity of what is done by bills of exchange in the matter of the assignment of debt. Of course, neither common law nor equity can supply ready means of giving increased value to instruments by the addition of names. You know a bill of exchange becomes exceedingly valuable by every name that is added to it, and it is by the simple addition of a name by way of indorsement that credit is increased and that a bill of exchange with several names on the back becomes so valuable. It is thus that bills of exchange are so readily accepted as real marketable commodities, and can be used with great facility for carrying out mercantile transactions.

Now you will learn still, if you open your books, that a chose in action, or a debt, is not assignable at common law. Well, that is only so in words, because an assignee of a debt could always sue at common law in the name of the assignor, and an assignment of the debt itself impliedly confers an authority on the assignee to use the assignor's name in all legal proceedings for the purpose of recovering the debt, subject to indemnifying him against the cost of the proceedings. Still further, the law courts have by their decisions taken care to enable the assignee to carry on the action for his own benefit. Take an instance. I had a case in which the assignor, after having assigned the debt, released the debt, and to an action brought in the assignor's name the debtor pleaded the release. This seemed to offer a great obstacle to the success of the action. The same judges that had said that a chose in action was not assignable had taken every care that in practice it should. What I had to do was to go to a judge at Chambers and ask him to strike out the plea on the ground that the release was fraudulent between the plaintiff, the assignor, and the defendant, telling him I was acting for a client who was the assignee and real owner of the debt and was truly the plaintiff. He struck the plea of release out accordingly, and judgment was entered for the plaintiff for want of a plea. Suppose, for instance, the assignor of a debt, after the assignment, became bankrupt, and the assignee commenced an action against the debtor in the name

of the assignor, the debtor might plead the bankruptcy
of the creditor, which would show *primâ facie* that the
debt was not in the plaintiff but in his trustee in
bankruptcy. The plaintiff would reply that the debt
had been assigned *bonâ fide* and for value prior to the
bankruptcy. This would be an answer to the plea,
because the trustee in bankruptcy takes only what
the bankrupt is both legally and beneficially entitled
to, and this replication shows that the plaintiff, at the
time of the bankruptcy, had no beneficial interest in
the debt, and the debt had consequently not passed
to the trustee but remained in the plaintiff. If the
replication was true in fact, judgment would be given
for the plaintiff, of which judgment the assignee of
the debt could alone avail himself. It is from these
arrangements, many and complicated, you learn that
even at law a chose in action can be assigned. The
Chancery judges, on the other hand, openly decided
that a chose in action could be assigned, and allowed
the assignee to sue for the debt in his own name,
making both the assignor and the debtor parties to the
proceedings. The Chancery judges thus conferred
great benefits on the community. Therefore, you see
that some of the powers in respect to the assignment
of debt incident to a bill of exchange were in existence
under the common law and the law of the Court of
Chancery, and which powers still exist.

Then I want to show you, that although these
powers in respect of an assignment of debt still
exist, what advantages the assignee of a debt
obtains by means of the indorsement of a bill of
exchange. The indorsee need not give any notice to
any parties to the bill that he has taken the bill in order
to obtain the full advantage of it. He does not
know or care whether the acceptor knows of the indorsement to him or not; he does not ask, and need
not ask, the acceptor whether he owes the money; he
gives him no notice of any kind. He does not regard
the acceptor in the slightest; and even if there may

have been fraud or failure of consideration in any of the dealings of the previous parties to the bill, if he is a *bonâ fide* holder for value, he will be entitled to sue all antecedent parties. Look at the advantages of bills of exchange in the matter of the assignment of debt, and how they contrast with transactions of assignment of debt at common law and in equity. A person in equity can assign a debt to anyone for value by any words that indicate that the one shall part with and the other become the owner of the debt; but to be safe, the assignee must give notice to the debtor of the assignment, for if he should not, and the creditor should make an assignment for value of the same debt to a second assignee without notice of the previous assignment, such second assignee, giving notice to the debtor before the first assignee does so, would become the owner of the debt as against the first assignee.

Now, nothing of that sort can arise with respect to a bill of exchange, and the indorsee of a bill of exchange is not under any obligation to give the slightest notice of any kind to the persons whose names appear on the bill that he has become indorsee of the bill.

There is another advantage which attaches to the indorsee of a bill of exchange, who becomes such before the bill matures, viz., that if he is the *bonâ fide* holder for value he does not take the instrument subject to any equity of any kind subsisting between any of the previous parties to the bill; whereas, you know that if a man is the assignee of a chose in action he always has to take the chance of the position of the person who has given him the security or assigned to him the debt. You will find the doctrine established and illustrated in a magnificent judgment of Lord St. Leonards, then Lord Chancellor, in the case of *Mangles* v. *Dixon*, a decision which you will find in 3 House of Lords, p. 702. You will there find an accurate and admirably expressed statement of the equitable doctrines with respect to the assignment of a chose in action, and the extent to which an assignee of a chose in action is affected by the equities existing between the assignor of the debt and the debtor. It is pleasant to read the satirical references of the Lord Chancellor to common law lawyers labouring to apply a half apprehended equity. It is worth noticing that in 1852 there was little waste of judicial power. In the case of *Mangles* v. *Dixon*, the Lord Chancellor, sitting by himself, in the House of Lords, reversed the decision of Lord Cottenham delivered when Chancellor, and reinstated the decision of Vice-Chancellor Knight Bruce which Lord Cottenham had reversed. But although the rule in equity is that the assignee of a chose in action takes it subject to the equities subsisting between the assignor and his debtor, yet the Chancery judges have gone a step further in facilitating the assignment of debt by allowing a debtor to agree by the instrument that creates the debt that the person who takes the instrument by assignment from the creditor shall take it unaffected by any equities between himself and his creditor. If you follow me, this is coming very near to the power which is attained by the indorsement of a bill of exchange, but there is this further thing which has never yet been reached by the rules of equity as to assignment of debt, that the indorsee of a bill of exchange for value is entitled to the amount upon the bill as against all precedent parties to the instrument, even although there has been fraud or deceit in the inception or transfer of the bill or no real transaction to which the instrument relates.

My time is up. I will proceed on the next occasion to call your attention shortly to the various parties that appear upon the face of specimen papers which will be laid before you.

No. 1.

LONDON, *February 1st, 1895.*

£100 : 0 : 0.

On demand
At sight

Three months after date pay to my Order the sum of One Hundred Pounds, value received.

WILLIAM SMITH.

To
JAMES ROBINSON,
52, Old Change,
London.

BILLS OF EXCHANGE.

No. 2.

£100:0:0.

London, *February 1st*, 1895.

Three months after date pay to my Order the sum of One Hundred Pounds, value received.

Accepted; Payable at
Barclay, Bevan & Co.,
Lombard Street,
London.

JAMES ROBINSON.

WILLIAM SMITH.

To
JAMES ROBINSON,
52, Old Change,
London.

No. 3.

LONDON, *February 1st,* 1895.

Three months after date pay to my Order the sum of One Hundred Pounds, value received.

Accepted: payable at
Barclay, Bevan & Co.
Lombard Street
London

JAMES ROBINSON

To
JAMES ROBINSON,
52, Old Change,
London.

£100 : 0 : 0.

No. 4.

LONDON, *February 1st*, 1895.

£100 : 0 : 0.

Three months after date pay to James Johnson, or Order, the sum of One Hundred Pounds, value received.

To
JAMES ROBINSON,
52, Old Change,
London.

WILLIAM SMITH.

*Accepted, payable at
Barclay, Bevan & Co.,
Lombard
Street
London.
JAMES ROBINSON.*

No. 5.

LONDON, *February 1st, 1895.*

£100 : 0 : 0.

Three months after date pay to James Johnson, or Bearer, the sum of One Hundred Pounds, value received.

To
JAMES ROBINSON,
52, Old Change,
London.

WILLIAM SMITH.

Accepted; payable at
Barclay, Bevan & Co.
Lombard Street
London

JAMES ROBINSON

No. 6.

LONDON, 30 *December*, 1809.

Two months after date pay to my Order £15 for value received.

F. JACKSON.

132, Oxford Street
payable at Mr. Hudson's
Accepted, Jo. HUDSON
Accepted, IRVING

To
MR. J. IRVING.

BILLS OF EXCHANGE. 91

No. 7.

May 20th, 1813.

Two months after date pay to Me, or my Order, the sum of Thirty Pounds Two Shillings.

W. SUSTANANCE.

Accepted
CHARLES WILNER.

Payable at No. 1, Wilmot Street,
Bethnal Green,
London.

BILLS OF EXCHANGE. 93

No. 8.

London, 8th March, 1838.

Twelve months after date pay to Me or my Order, One Hundred Pounds, payable at 319, Strand, value received.

JOHN HART.

Accepted
H. J. Clarke

To
Mr. John Hart.

£100.

No. 9.

London, *March 24th*, 1860.

Two months after date pay to Mrs. Emma Fielder, or Order, Thirty-five Pounds, value received.

To
Mrs. Emma Fielder,
Trafalgar Square,
Chelsea.

Accepted; payable at
50, King William Street, City.
Samuel Marshall.

ANN LANGSTAFFE.

LECTURE IV.

On the last occasion when I spoke to you, I told you that in my view it was better for you to try and ascertain what transactions at common law could not be the subject of bills of exchange or promissory notes, and what transactions could be carried out by bills of exchange or promissory notes, which could not be effected either by the principles of common law or the Courts of Equity; and that if you carefully studied those transactions you would soon have in your minds a true definition of a "bill of exchange" or "promissory note," without committing to memory the definition you find in the Act of Parliament of 1882, which professes to codify the law relating to bills of exchange. I also called your attention to the most important incident to a bill of exchange, namely : how it secured the assignment of debt in a safe and simple manner. I also, at the close of my last address, very hurriedly called your attention to two cases, the names of which I am afraid I did not give you, but which I want you to have, because it is worth while seeing how far the Judges of the Court of Equity have gone in endeavouring to do in the matter of the assignment of debt some portion of that which is effected by a bill of exchange. You remember I told you that in equity, a *chose in action* or a debt could be assigned like any other property, and that the person to whom it was assigned could sue for the recovery of the debt in his own name. I told you also, that the assignee of the debt took it subject to all the equities subsisting between the assignor and the debtor, but that the Courts of Equity had gone thus far: that they had laid it down that a person might agree to contract himself out of the right to assert as against the assignee of a creditor, equities which would be available against the creditor. Whether a debtor has done so depends upon the true construction of the words he has used. In one case the Court may say the debtor has done so; in another, that he has not. Notwithstanding, therefore, the rule just mentioned, the assignee of the debt, except in a very clear case, can never be sure he is free from the equities attaching to the debt. From all such doubt and risk the transferee of a bill of exchange is altogether and absolutely free, if endorsed to him before maturity. The law of the Courts of Equity upon this point, and the different constructions put by judges on the words employed by the debtor, may be well studied in the decision of Lord Justice Rolt in the case of *In re Blakely Ordnance Company*, at p. 154, and the decision of Lord Cairns in the case of *In re The Natal Investment Co.*, at p. 355 of the third volume of Law Rep., Chancery Appeals.

I call your attention to those judgments in order to show you how Judges may differ as to the true meaning of the contract into which the debtor has entered, and may differ as to whether or not the party entering into the obligation has agreed that he will not avail himself as against an assignee, of any equities he may be able to assert against the person with whom he is contracting. These two cases will show you how difficult it is to tell whether the debtor or obligor has entered into such an engagement. In the one case, Lord Justice Rolt held, that the debtor had so contracted; in the other, Lord Cairns decided that he had not, overruling a decision of the Master of the Rolls, who had arrived at the conclusion that the debtor had so contracted. With respect, however, to bills of exchange or promissory notes, a person in trade or business incurs no such difficulty or risk. If he takes the instrument honestly, and for value and without notice, he is unaffected by anything transpiring between the previous parties to the instrument; neither is he troubled with equities, nor with any contract into which the prior parties or any of them may have entered.

I also forgot to tell you, when stating in respect of bills of exchange, that at every stage the presumption is that it has always been dealt with or parted with for consideration, that it is always open to a party to establish that there really was no consideration for the acceptance or indorsement of the bill, and then, of course, if the claim is between immediate parties, no action will lie; and if the acceptor could sustain the same allegation between all the subsequent parties to the instrument, he will have an answer to any action brought upon the instrument, and no liability will exist in respect of it.

When I first of all attended a lecture on bills of exchange and promissory notes, I had the advantage of having been familiar with their use whilst I was engaged in business in the City; but a young man present on that occasion said to me: "I do not understand a word that has been said because I have never seen such an instrument, and I scarcely know to what the lecturer is referring. I hear the words 'drawer,' 'drawee,' 'acceptor'; I have never heard them before, and I really have carried away this morning no clear and definite views of the instrument to which the lecturer has been calling our attention." Remembering the difficulty my fellow-student then experienced, I have taken the trouble to have certain lithographic forms* prepared, which you will find upon the tables. These I desire you to take and keep.

Now, if the Lord Chief Justice of England will allow me to give him a set of the forms, and to say how cheered

---

* *The forms placed before the gentlemen attending the lecture are found printed on the pages preceding this lecture.*

we all are by his presence to-night, I will proceed at once to call your attention to No. 1 of the specimen instruments. No. 1 is a perfect bill of exchange. I do not mean to say that there may not be other names added, but it is in its present state a bill of exchange. It contains, as you will see, on the right-hand corner, the name of a particular person. Understand me, it is not requisite that this form should be observed; but as I have practised at the Bar now thirty years, and have never seen any different form, you need not trouble yourselves much with some of those strange instruments which, fifty, sixty, or eighty years ago, troubled the Courts, and were drawn by persons who had but little intelligence. The schoolmaster has been abroad. As I was saying, you will find in the right-hand bottom corner, the name of "William Smith." He is the drawer of this instrument, and always keep that word to describe his part in the transaction. Now, if you notice, he requests that somebody will, three months after date, pay to his order the sum of £100. He, William Smith, therefore, is the drawer of the instrument. It is addressed to "James Robinson, 52, Old Change, London." His name is in the left-hand corner of the bill. He is the drawee. Keep that word as the word which signifies the person to whom the instrument is addressed, viz., the drawee. Use it then for that purpose and for no other. As I have said, "William Smith" is the drawer. Then I can tell you, upon the authority of Mr. Justice Patteson in the case of *Davis* v. *Clarke*, reported in 13 L. J. Q. B., p. 305, that an instrument like No. 1 (properly stamped, of course) constitutes a perfect bill of exchange, although you must have already noticed that there is no acceptance upon this instrument. Just notice that, please—there is no acceptor to this instrument No. 1, but only drawer and drawee. No doubt you remember that, in early times, an instrument such as this, a bill of exchange, was used for the purpose of providing money in distant places to discharge obligations arising there, and the bill of exchange, therefore, was generally drawn and circulated before ever it was accepted. Let me illustrate what I mean. One man comes to another in London, and says, "I want to pay a debt in Florence; does anybody there owe you any money?" "Yes," is the reply. "How much?" "£200." "That is the sum I want; then will you draw upon your debtor in Florence for the £200, payable to the order of my creditor, and give the instrument to me?" "I will." "How much do you want for it?"—So much. The money is paid, the bill is drawn as requested and handed over, and the debtor sends it to his creditor in Florence, who procures the acceptance of the bill and, at maturity, the money. The instrument before acceptance was a perfect bill of exchange, and was dealt with as such.

On the other hand, bear in mind that you cannot have a bill of exchange without a drawer, and for that you find an excellent authority in the case of *Peto* v. *Reynolds*, which is reported in 9 Exchequer Reports, p. 410. There you will find Baron Parke saying, except in one case of *Regina* v. *Hawkes*, 2 Moody's Crown Cases, p. 60, there is no case in the books which establishes that there can be a bill of exchange without the existence of two parties, the drawer and the drawee.

Now let us proceed. This bill, No. 1, as you notice, is an "inland" bill of exchange. It is drawn by one man in London upon another man in London. I have not had time to ascertain whether it be so now, but it is quite certain from an examination of the works of Pothier, that a bill of exchange in his time, in France, was not valid if it was drawn by one person upon another person living and residing in the same town. I think Article 111, Code de Commerce, shows that the law of France on the subject is still the same as in the time of Pothier. The instrument, in order to be valid as a bill of exchange, must have been drawn by a person in one town upon some person residing in another town. That is not the law of our country, and a bill drawn by one person residing in London upon another person residing in London, or a bill drawn by one person residing in Manchester upon another person residing in Manchester is a perfectly good instrument; no objection to it as a bill of exchange can be taken on the ground of the drawer and drawee residing in the same place. Another thing I should tell you is this. It is not necessary to the validity of a bill of exchange that there should be the place of business or residence either of the drawer or of the acceptor, or any place at all; nor even that it should be stated where the instrument is payable. Next, it is not necessary that there should be a date to the instrument. It is a perfectly good bill of exchange without any date. The date can be proved, and the date may be filled in; and if a holder for value honestly fills it in, making a mistake as to the date, it is none the less a good instrument; and if it has been filled in with a date before it comes to a person who is a *bonâ fide* holder for value, no possible objection can be taken to it on the ground that the date has been improperly filled in.

Now let me pass on. The next thing you get is the £100 in figures. I have told you before that a bill of exchange must be for a precise amount of money. It must fix the relation of debtor and creditor. It must be £100, or some other definite amount—£100, or whatever the amount is, and nothing else—not £100, and an obligation to pledge goods; not £100, or the delivery of certain goods in lieu of the £100. It must be a precise sum of money that is the subject of the drawing. It may, however, be payable by instalments. You may have the £100, in the body of it payable by instalments, and you may have, if you like, a proviso that on the non-payment of any one instalment the whole shall become due and payable.

But now I must tell you that the figures on a bill are controlled by the words of the bill. If you notice, in the bill as I have drawn it, there is "£100" in figures and "One Hundred Pounds" in words. I will here give you the names of two cases, both of which are worthy of your study. The first is the case of *Sanderson* v. *Piper*, reported in 5 Bingham's New Cases, p. 431. In that case the figures were "£250" and the words in the body of the instrument "Two Hundred Pounds." Held, that the bill was only good for £200, and not for £250. Then, in the case of *Garrard* v. *Lewis*, reported in 10 Queen's Bench Division, p. 30, the late Lord Bowen, then Lord Justice Bowen, sitting as a judge of first instance, decided that until the words are filled in, in the body of the instrument, the instrument in question is not a bill. His Lordship does not say that if there are no figures in the margin it is not a bill—quite the contrary ; nor do I understand him to say, that if in the body of the instrument instead of "One Hundred Pounds" being in words the "£100" is in figures, that that would not be a good bill. There are two or three cases that I could give you in which, as far as I can judge, there were no figures at all in the margin of the instrument, the amount was not given in words, but the amount was put in figures in the body of the instrument, and it was held to be, and must be held to be, a good bill of exchange. But in the case of *Garrard* v. *Lewis*, Lord Bowen adopted this view, that the words so far controlled the figures that the figures themselves are not a material part of the instrument, and that the fact of their having been altered does not constitute a material alteration of the instrument so as to avoid the bill.

Now, the next thing I want to call attention to is this. I have drawn this bill, No. 1, in this form :— "Three months after date pay to my order." That is a perfectly good, common form. It may sometimes be, "Pay to me or my order." Now I want to tell you the importance of those few words. If you look at writers such as Pothier, he tells you that you cannot have a bill of exchange unless there are three parties to the instrument—drawer, drawee, and a payee, as distinct from the drawer. Let me illustrate it in this way: When, for instance, a person wanted to send money to a distant town, he said to the person whose bill he was getting, "Draw it upon your correspondent in favour of the person whose debt I want to discharge;" so that a bill of exchange drawn in London upon a person in Florence, payable to a person in Florence, on being paid by the acceptor would discharge the debt which he owed to the drawer, and, the bill being made payable to the creditor, would, as soon as that money reached his hands discharge the debt due to him from the person who procured and forwarded the bill. You would have in that case drawer, drawee, payee. According to the law of France when Pothier wrote, although the French law now is in conformity with the English in this respect, there must be these three parties to the instrument in order that it might be a bill of exchange. Our law has not required the existence of three persons. By our law the drawer may be himself the payee. You see the importance of this difference to the trade of this country. When a man is in business, and he sells a parcel of goods amounting in the whole, say, to £175, he may have no person in his mind to whom he wants to pass the bill on the day he draws it, but he desires to have a bill of exchange in his possession, ready for use whenever necessary. He therefore draws the bill payable to his order. See the wisdom with which our Judges have built up our law following all the needs of commerce itself. They have held that such an instrument is a valid bill of exchange. So that now you may have an instrument, "Pay to me or my order." A trader does not want to use the bill to-day, nay, he may wait until perhaps he gets £20,000 or £30,000 worth of such bills, good trade bills, and then he takes them to a bill broker or to his bankers for discount. He gets the money value of the bills, meets his engagements, and carries on, let us hope, a successful business. I would refer you in this connection to the case of *Re Stoltz*, which is reported in 6 Modern Reports, p. 29. The decision in that case that those simple words " me or my order " made " a good bill of exchange" was a most important decision for the trade and business of this country. Now, of course, you may have a bill drawn thus : " Pay to bearer." I had not time to have a lithographed form for every possible instrument; but you can write the words " or bearer" over the words "or order," in No. 1.

Now if you notice I have put upon the form No. 1, " Three months after date." That is three months from the 1st February. You might have " Three months after sight," and that means three months from the time when the bill is presented for acceptance. It is legally seen at sight whenever it is presented for acceptance, and if it is not accepted it is dishonoured, upon which proceedings can at once be taken against the person from whom the bill was received. You can write "sight," over " date." Now you can also have the bill drawn payable " on demand," and a bill of exchange of course would be payable on demand where the words are " on demand," or if there is no time mentioned at all it would be payable on demand; or, if it is payable " at sight " or payable " on presentation," the bill of exchange would then be payable on demand. I hurry forward because most of the things I am now mentioning you will find in the provisions of the Act of 1882 ; but I am anxious to talk to you in a plain, simple way, so that having heard me you may be able to avail yourselves of its provisions in any emergency.

Now there is another thing I must mention. No. 1 is an " inland " bill of exchange. An inland bill of exchange has been defined long since. An inland bill of exchange is one that either is or purports to be drawn within the British Isles and payable therein, or one which is actually drawn within the British Isles upon a person resident therein, even although it may be payable out of the United Kingdom. This is the definition of an " inland " bill of exchange, and every other instrument outside this definition is a "foreign" bill of exchange.

Now let me tell you that you can have two persons or more as drawers, drawees, and acceptors, and they need not be partners. You may have three or four if you like, but you cannot have them successively or alternatively; it must be addressed to them jointly as if they were one person. Then I need scarcely tell you that anyone accepting will be liable as acceptor although the other drawees do not accept. Keep these simple views in your mind and you will have very little difficulty in dealing with such an instrument. You may, of course, have two or more persons drawing, but they must constitute as it were one drawer, or you may have two or three persons, as persons to whom the bill is addressed, but you cannot have them successively or alternatively— it must be addressed to one or more persons constituting, as it were, one drawee of the instrument.

There is another thing which it is important for you young men to remember, because I have seen mistakes made by reason of forgetting it. This bill No. 1 is drawn without any acceptance thereon. It has a drawee, but as yet it has not been accepted. I shall hereafter have to discuss with you the passing of a promissory note or bill of exchange by indorsement or delivery. Suppose, then, the first specimen bill, No. 1, has been passed away through five or six hands and at length it is taken to Mr. Robinson at Old Change and he refuses to accept; who can sue Mr. Robinson for not accepting? Only the person who can say that Mr. Robinson has agreed with him to accept the bill. Therefore remember that if you take a bill without acceptance you, the holder of it, can sue the drawer and all intermediate indorsers; and of course if you have several good names on the bill it may be almost as good as a Bank of England note. Still you have no action against the drawee if he does not accept,

and if by chance you have taken the bill because it is
drawn upon a responsible person from a drawer who is
a man without means, you may find yourself ultimately
in the possession of a piece of paper of little or no
value. As a general rule the only person who can sue
the drawee for non-acceptance is the drawer, and in
specimen No. 1 he is William Smith; but then William
Smith cannot sue for non-acceptance unless Mr.
Robinson has agreed to accept. William Smith may
still, however, resort to the consideration for the bill,
viz., goods sold and delivered or money lent, but he
cannot sue Robinson for not accepting this bill unless
there has been a promise to do so. I hurry over
these matters because I have to comprise all I have
to say on negotiable securities in only a few lectures.

Now the next specimen is No. 2. Here you will
find that the bill has been accepted, and you see
"Accepted; payable at Barclay, Bevan & Co., Lombard
Street, London : James Robinson," written across the
face of the instrument. Now that is the ordinary form
in which a bill is accepted. Let me tell you that
prior to the 1st & 2nd George IV. cap. 78, a bill of
exchange might be accepted by word of mouth. I
need not stay to trouble you with cases which show
the disadvantages of such a state of the law. Since
the 1st & 2nd George IV. cap. 78, the acceptance
of an inland bill of exchange must be in writing
on the instrument or on some one part of the instrument if it is drawn in two, three, or four bills constituting a set. The law continued unaltered with
respect to foreign bills of exchange down to the 19th
& 20th Vict. cap. 97, but from that time forward the
acceptance of a "foreign" bill of exchange must be
in writing either on the bill itself, or on one of the
four bills which, as a rule, make the set in the
case of a "foreign" bill of exchange. Every acceptance, therefore, now of a bill of exchange must be in
writing.

There was a great discussion many years ago

as to what was the effect of an acceptance payable at a particular place, such as that you read on No. 2:—"Accepted; payable at Barclay, Bevan & Co., Lombard Street, London; James Robinson." Was that a general acceptance or a qualified acceptance? That is to say, in order to charge the acceptor with the non-payment of this instrument were you bound to present it for payment at Barclay, Bevan & Co.? The question was set at rest by that very same Act, 1st & 2nd Geo. IV. cap. 78, which enacted that an acceptance like the one you see on the second form should not be deemed a qualified acceptance at all, but a general acceptance, with respect to place. I shall have to shew you that you can have a qualified acceptance with respect to everything almost, except as to the way in which the bill shall be paid. You cannot have a qualified acceptance to pay the bill in goods, or in services; but with these exceptions you can have the bill accepted conditionally in all manner of ways. The Act of Parliament above mentioned provides that no acceptance shall be deemed to be a qualified acceptance as to place, unless the acceptor shall in his acceptance express that he accepts the bill payable at a banker's house or other place "only and not otherwise or elsewhere." If you find these words as part of the acceptance, then you cannot charge the acceptor unless you have presented the bill for payment at Barclay, Bevan & Co., or any other place at which the acceptor may have made the bill payable. You need not present it at once or any fixed day. Presentation at any time within six years will be sufficient to charge the acceptor. Mind you, I am not speaking of charging the drawer, indorser, or payee, but with respect to charging the acceptor. At any time you can present the bill at the place mentioned on the instrument, and you will have a perfectly good cause of action against the acceptor if the bill is not honoured; but you will have no cause of action against him until you do so present it.

Now let me say again that it is not necessary

to have such a formal acceptance as appears on No. 2. "Accepted, James Robinson," would be perfectly good. On a certain day, in a moment of forgetfulness which comes even to the most brilliant intellects when they are on the bench, some judges, quite forgetting previous decisions, decided that James Robinson did not accept a bill if he merely put "Accepted; James Robinson." To correct the mistake, an Act of Parliament was passed, the 41 Vict. cap. 13. By this Act it is enacted that the word "accepted" and a name shall be a perfectly good acceptance. But long before this Act it had been decided that if you had a name across a bill answering to the name of the drawee, without the word "accepted," that would be a perfectly good acceptance; and so now, under the Act of 1882, you can have four forms: "James Robinson;" "Accepted; James Robinson;" "Accepted; payable at Barclay, Bevan & Co., bankers, Lombard Street;" and then, lastly, the fourth, "Accepted; payable at Barclay, Bevan & Co. only, not elsewhere and not otherwise." Keep these distinctions in your minds and you will be able to deal with the various instruments as they come before you.

Now just let me ask you for a moment to take in your hands specimen No. 3—you find there is no drawer's name: William Smith's name is not there, as on No. 1 and No. 2—and assume, if you please, that all the rest is on the instrument, addressed to "James Robinson, Old Change, London"; "Accepted; payable at Barclay, Bevan & Co., Lombard Street, London; James Robinson." Now I should like you to take the view which I generally adopt for myself, viz., that the specimen No. 3 is not an instrument of any kind. You find that in No. 3 you have no name of a drawer, and as I have told you, it cannot, therefore, be a bill of exchange. For a bill of exchange, you must have a drawer. I do not like to speak of it, when I wish to avoid all error, even as an acceptance in blank or an inchoate bill, although both these terms are applied to such a document. In the state in which you see it, it is not worth more than the paper on which the words are written. When a drawer's name is lawfully placed upon it, it will become a bill of exchange, and the words across the face of it will become an acceptance. The calling such a document as this by the right name may be of practical importance in other cases than those in which an action may be brought upon such a document. Thus, some few years ago an action was brought against a railway company for the loss of goods, and a claim was made for the loss of nine sovereigns. The company said they were not responsible for their loss, because the parcel contained gold and securities to the value of £20. A railway company, as you all know, is not responsible for gold and other securities above the value of £10, unless notice of the contents of the parcel has been given to them. The parcel contained nine sovereigns, and an instrument exactly like specimen No. 3. No notice of the contents had been given. The instrument had been given by the person who wrote the words across the face of it for goods sold and delivered to him, with an authority, of course, to the vendor to fill up the bill with his name as drawer. When the instrument was received by the railway company there was no drawer's name upon it. The Court held that the parcel contained gold and securities only to the extent of £9, because the instrument was not a security at all, and was in its then state nothing more than a piece of paper, and of no pecuniary value at all; and that the plaintiff was entitled to recover for the loss of the nine sovereigns. *Sloessiger* v. *South Eastern Railway Company*, 3 Ellis and Blackburn, p. 549.

I desire to call your attention to other cases, which show what an essential part of a bill the drawing is. There have been three very important cases on this matter. Let me just give you one, *Ex parte Haywood*, *re Haywood*, L. R. 6 Chan. Ap. 546. The question arose on a petition in bankruptcy. A creditor says: "I have a bill of exchange accepted by the person against whom the petition is presented; he has not met the bill. He has committed an act of bankruptcy. I want him adjudicated a bankrupt." "Oh," says an intelligent young junior, just called, full of learning, "Sir, an order of adjudication cannot properly be made. This bill of exchange, it is true, bears date the 17th March; true, the assignment for the benefit of creditors was on the 4th of April, upon which reliance is placed as an act of bankruptcy; the act of bankruptcy is subsequent to the date of this bill. It is drawn, sir, I admit; it is a perfect instrument; but I propose to show you that although the acceptor's name was put on the instrument on the 17th of March the drawer's name was not put there until the 24th of May." "Oh," says the Registrar, "what has that to do with it? He has committed an act of bankruptcy, and he accepted the bill prior thereto. I shall make him a bankrupt." Lord Justice James and Lord Justice Mellish, when the case is brought before them, say: "Oh, no; there never was a bill of exchange at all until the 24th of May, when the drawer's name was put to it." "Oh, but it became a bill of exchange at the date of the bill, because the drawing relates back to the date of the acceptance," says the counsel for the petitioning creditor. Reply: "No, there is no relation backwards; the drawing cannot relate back to the date of the acceptance. That instrument never had any existence as a bill until the 24th of May, when it was drawn, nor was the person against whom the petition is presented an acceptor until then. The act of bankruptcy was committed on the 4th of April, at a time when the petitioning creditor was not a creditor at all. And as the petitioning creditor's debt must be subsisting at the time of the act of bankruptcy, the adjudication must be annulled." You know how men smile when you talk in Court of elementary principles, forgetting that almost every case in Court is determined by the application of some elementary principle, which, if stated at the beginning of the argument, none would dispute.

In the case of *Baxendale* v. *Bennett*, reported in Law Reports, 3 Queen's Bench Div., p. 525, you will see the importance of ascertaining when and how the instrument came to have a drawer's name upon it. In that case the defendant put his name as acceptor across the face of a piece of paper with a bill stamp upon it for the purpose of raising money. A drawer's name was not upon it. He put the piece of paper in his desk, and one day left his desk open. Somebody took the paper out, and filled it up with a drawer's name. It got into the hands of a *bonâ fide* holder for value. Held, the *bonâ fide* holder could not recover; that this paper never had any existence as a bill of exchange by the authority of the person who had put his name across it as if he would become an acceptor. Read that case, study it, and you will be in possession of all the learning bearing on this question.

Now take another case in the same volume of Reports, the case of *Hogarth* v. *Latham*, p. 643; and there you will see that a man who puts words across an instrument that is stamped, purporting to accept, and parts with it without the amount being filled up and without a drawer's name to the instrument, may find, if he has authorised such person to become drawer or to permit anyone else to become the drawer, that he has clothed the person to whom he has surrendered the document with authority to fill it up to the largest amount of money the stamp will cover. But if a person, however honestly, takes a piece of paper on which an acceptor's name appears but no drawer's name, then, according to the authorities as I read them, he runs the risk of the person who gives him the instrument not having authority to allow a drawer's name to be put to the instrument. If it turns out that authority to put a drawer's name has been given, then no question arises; but if not, then the instrument has not become a bill of exchange, and the person who has put his name across it as acceptor cannot be made liable as acceptor. If, when you take what is called a blank acceptance from any person other than the so-called acceptor, you see that there is no drawer's name there, and you are going to put your name as drawer or ask somebody else to become the drawer, then it will be at your risk whether what is being done is done with the sanction of the person who has put these words, "Accepted payable," across the piece of paper. Read, therefore, the last two cases that I have given you, and those of you who are engaged in business will see at once the importance of never taking without enquiry an instrument on which there is not a drawer's name. Of course, you cannot tell when it is already filled up whether any wrong has been done; but if you find there is no drawer's name filled in, then you run the risk of whatever is done in the way of drawing the bill, not having been done with the authority of the person who has put his name across the instrument.

Now the acceptance I have told you may be qualified or conditional; the drawing never can be. It seems by the law of France there cannot even be a conditional acceptance. Supposing you draw for £100 payable out of the proceeds of certain goods to be sold, that is not a bill of exchange. Suppose you draw for £100 payable on realization of a cargo, that is also not a bill of exchange. Suppose you draw for £100 payable on the arrival of a vessel, that is not a good bill. Suppose you draw for £100, but tell the drawee he may pay himself out of a particular fund, that is a good bill. Suppose you draw for £100, and tell the drawee to charge it to a certain account, the instrument is still a bill of exchange. Suppose you draw for £100, stating the reason for drawing it, namely, " pursuant to a memorandum," that is still a good bill. Those are good bills, but if you have either an uncertain amount of money, or you have a certain amount with an obligation to do something more than to pay the money, or you have a contingency of the kind I have expressed annexed to the drawing, there is no bill. Remember, also, you cannot have a contingency as to the time for the payment of the money—"Pay three months after Caius shall return from Rome" would not be a good bill. If it were three months after the happening of an event, although uncertain as to time, but one that is sure to happen, it would nevertheless be a good bill. Therefore, if it were "three months after the death of A. B.," it would be a perfectly good bill. Just keep those things in your minds. On the other hand do not forget this, that you can have a qualified acceptance. A man can say: "Yes, I accept, payable when I have realized a cargo;" or "I accept payable on the giving up certain bills of lading to me;" or, "I accept payable on being put in funds at a particular bank by a certain day." An acceptor may qualify his acceptance almost in any way he likes, and if such an acceptance is taken it is a perfectly good acceptance. I will speak in a moment of the obligation of the person who takes a qualified acceptance to give notice to the previous parties to the instrument that he has done so, but it is a perfectly good acceptance, if it is taken. Now, you can have a bill drawn for £100, and the drawee may accept for £50. Understand that. He can change the place and time. He can accept (apart from the question of stamp duty), at three months although the bill is drawn at two months. Therefore never forget that whilst an acceptance may be under all conditions almost, and under all circumstances, qualified in every way except as to the method of paying, there can be no qualification as to the drawing; there must be an unconditional request. You will meditate upon this distinction. No condition can enter into the drawing of a bill of exchange, but the acceptance may be conditional in the various ways which I have mentioned to you.

Having told you this, I must now say to you that a man who holds a bill as indorsee, and who is going to take a qualified acceptance, will take it at his own risk. "To be sure, what business have you to take a qualified acceptance?" the drawer may say to him. The holder takes it at his own risk, and he will thereby discharge all the parties previous to himself if the acceptance is not taken with their authority, express or implied; but if he informs them of his having taken the qualified acceptance, and they do not express their dissent to the holder within a reasonable time, they will be deemed to have assented thereto. Therefore at once you must inform the prior parties to the bill, if you take a conditional acceptance, of what you have done, and if they do not dissent, the acceptance will be binding, and they will still continue liable upon the bill. Of course, a qualified acceptance offered by the drawee may be refused, and the holder who can only get a qualified acceptance may treat the bill as dishonoured by non-acceptance, and at once render all previous parties liable.

Now I desire to call your attention to a bill drawn in favour of a payee. Take specimen No. 4. "Three months after date pay to James Johnson or order." This is the convenient way, if you want to discharge an obligation to Mr. Johnson, of drawing the bill. There is one thing I ought to tell you here—that I think the Act of 1882 has changed the law with respect to a point arising in connection with a bill drawn in favour of a payee. Suppose a bill had been drawn thirty or forty years ago, "Three months after date pay James Johnson," that would have been held to be an instrument not transferable, because it is not said to be to the order of James Johnson; but now under the Act of 1882, where a bill is made payable to a particular individual, without saying to his order, and there are no words restricting the transfer of the instrument, then the instrument is as transferable as if it had been drawn payable to the man and his order. Therefore you may take it from me, that if the specimen No. 4 had been drawn, "Three months after date pay to James Johnson," alone, that would, since 1882, have been an instrument capable of transfer; and James Johnson (by a method which we shall discuss, I hope, at our next lecture, when I come to speak to you about the passing of property in bills of exchange and promissory notes) could pass it as readily and freely as the payee could in the specimen No. 4. You know that I have told you that at one time it was thought a bill of exchange must have a payee, but that is no longer necessary, at all events by the law of England, and a bill of exchange may be drawn to the order of the drawer. Then I have framed the next instrument, No. 5, as it appears payable to bearer, because it will be of service when I come to deal with the passing of property in a bill of exchange. There, as you will see, it is drawn payable to "James Johnson or bearer." I wish now to call your attention to specimen No. 6, because I want you to understand that no person can be an acceptor of a bill unless the bill has been addressed to him. See the importance of this in the case I am about to mention. Look, then, at specimen No. 6. Many of you, I dare say, at once will see the point, as you are more familiar with the cases than I am. Form No. 6 has been taken from the case of *Jackson* v. *Hudson*, reported in 2 Campbell, p. 447. You see the acceptance reads thus: "Accepted J. Irving; accepted Jos. Hudson, payable at Mr. Hudson's, 132, Oxford Street." You will notice upon this instrument, therefore, the names of two persons as acceptors. There is no objection in that form, because if the bill is addressed to two people in their separate names, not in the name of a partnership, their names must be put the one after the other. The objection taken before Lord Ellenborough was, that Mr. Hudson could not be sued as the acceptor, because he was not a drawee, not a person to whom the bill was addressed. Lord Ellenborough held that the objection was fatal, and ever since his day, it has been held that no person, no matter what words he uses, can be the acceptor of a bill unless he is a person to whom the bill has been addressed. It is addressed only to Irving, and not to Hudson. What was the position of Hudson? He was surety. Mr. Jackson would not sell his goods to Mr. Irving without having Hudson's undertaking to pay if Irving did not. Instead of drawing the bill on Hudson as well as Irving, which would have been perfectly in order, it is addressed only to "Irving," the parties, I have no doubt, thinking that if Hudson put his name as acceptor it imposed upon him the responsibility of acceptor. After this decision it is certain that the only action that would lie against Hudson would be an action upon a promise to indemnify Mr. Jackson against Mr. Irving's failing to pay for the goods that he purchased. That, as you know, would be an action of assumpsit sounding in damages, and you would have to show that the instrument signed by Hudson complied with the provisions of the 4th section of the Statute of Frauds, which requires such promise to be in writing. I do not say this instrument might not satisfy the statute. But do not let your clients or anybody for whom you are acting get into a position of doubt. Keep them in a straight, clear path; and if you know the law beforehand, you always will.

Having said thus much on Form No. 6, let me now pass to specimen No. 7. This is a very interesting case. I wonder (if I did not tell you) how long it would take you to find out the objection that was taken to this instrument. From it you will see that Mr. Sustanance draws the instrument and puts his name to it as drawer. Now see what he has written. Look at the left-hand corner, where you would expect to find the drawee's name. You do not find the name of any drawee; you only find, "Payable at No. 1, Wilmot Street, Bethnal Green, London." Then you will see across the face of the bill, "Accepted; Charles Milner." In an action brought against Charles Milner, as acceptor of the bill, to recover the sum for which it was drawn, an objection was taken that Charles Milner was not an acceptor because his name did not appear upon the instrument as a drawee. The Court held that before acceptance there was no drawee's name, but that as soon as Charles Milner put his name as acceptor, the words in the left-hand corner of the bill became definite and certain, and the acceptor acknowledged by his acceptance that he was the person to whom the bill was addressed. I am glad to tell you that it is the law of France and one or two other countries that instruments like the one you are now considering are perfectly good as acceptances. The case is reported under the name of *Gray* v. *Milner*, 8 Taunton's Reports, p. 739. The principle of it was stated in a subsequent case to be that a bill of exchange made payable at a particular place or house is meant to be addressed to the person who resides at that place, and if a man puts his name to it the presumption is, until the contrary appears, that he is the person residing there, and the person to whom it is addressed.

Now, if I may trespass upon your time for a moment or two longer than usual to-night, let me give you another illustration. I want to draw your attention to specimen No. 8. This specimen bill is a very important one. If you look at it you will see that John Hart is the drawer, and you will also see in the left-hand corner that John Hart is the drawee. John Hart has drawn upon himself. It has been placed now beyond all dispute that where a man draws upon himself the instrument is a perfectly good one, but it will be (at the election of the holder) either a promissory note or a bill of exchange. Treat John Hart as the drawer of a bill of exchange, and the holder may have to give him notice of dishonour in order to charge him. Treat him as a maker of a promissory note, and the holder will be free from all such obligation. So that if he says you have not given him notice of dishonour of the instrument so as to charge him as drawer you may say: "You drew upon yourself, and I, therefore, am entitled to consider the instrument either as a bill of exchange or as a promissory note; I treat it as a promissory note, and you, the maker, require no notice, and your obligation continues for six years from the time the instrument matured." But there is another and far more important matter to consider. Look and see how the instrument is accepted. It is: "Accepted, H. J. Clarke, payable at 319, Strand." Mr. Clarke was sued as acceptor. He took the objection that he was not the person upon whom the bill was drawn, and consequently could not become an acceptor and sued as an acceptor. It was assumed that John Hart and H. J. Clarke were different persons. This instrument is taken from the case of *Davis* v. *Clarke*, which is reported in 13 Law Journal, Queen's Bench, and in 6 Queen's Bench, p. 16. The Court decided that no action would lie against Clarke; he was not the acceptor of the instrument because it was not addressed to him, and it made no difference that Mr. John Hart, the person upon whom it was drawn, was one and the same person with the Mr. John Hart who drew it. Mr. Clarke, therefore, under that instrument could neither be made responsible as acceptor nor as the maker of a promissory note, and no obligation rested upon Mr. Clarke under the instrument.

Now let me pass on and deal with the next specimen, No. 9, and with its examination my address shall finish. This form is taken from the case of *Fielder* v. *Marshall*, reported in 9 Common Bench, New Series, p. 606. I should like you to try your judgment upon this instrument before I tell you about the question that arose and the decision at which the Court arrived. You see it is drawn by Ann Langstaffe, in favour of Mrs. Emma Fielder. Now in the corner what is there written?—" To Mrs. Emma Fielder, Trafalgar Square, Chelsea." Is that person the drawee? Then the acceptance is: " Accepted; payable at 50, King

William Street, City, Samuel Marshall." Samuel Marshall is sued, as the acceptor of the bill, by Emma Fielder, as the payee of the bill. The objection was taken that Samuel Marshall had never accepted any such bill, because he was not on the face of the instrument the drawee, or, in other words, the bill had never been addressed to him. Looking at the specimen, it is clear that Marshall is not the drawee, and could not become acceptor by anything he chose to write on the face of the instrument. The objection seems a good one. Then it was suggested for the plaintiff that if Marshall could not be sued as an acceptor, he could be sued as the maker of a promissory note. To this, answer was made that he might be so, if there were no drawee on the face of the bill; but that there was such a drawee, namely, Mrs. Emma Fielder, whose name you see in the left-hand corner of the instrument. The Court, however, came to the conclusion that Mrs. Fielder was not a drawee; that her address in the corner was not a direction of the bill to her, but a mere repetition of that which was contained in the body of the instrument, namely, that payment is to be made to her or her order. The Court said it was a case in which there was a direction to no one, and if the defendant could not be made liable as an acceptor he must be regarded as the maker of a promissory note. The plaintiff, therefore, recovered the full amount of the instrument.

I am obliged to you for the attention you have paid to me to-night. I trust that by the practical illustrations I have given you, the nature of a bill of exchange is rising clear in your minds otherwise than by a mere effort to recall the different definitions which others have prepared for you.

No. 10.

William Smith.

pay Thomas Daft (or Order),

James Richardson.

Thomas Daft.

William Hartley.

Mark Phillips.

pay James Saunders,

George French.

James Saunders.

pay William Robertson,

(Acceptor) James Robinson.

pay Jonathan George,

William Robertson.

No. 11.

LONDON, *January 1st, 1895.*

£100 : 0 : 0.

Three months after date pay at Barclay, Bevan & Co., to my Order, the sum of One Hundred Pounds, value received.

WILLIAM SMITH.

To
JAMES ROBINSON,
62, Old Change,
London.

LECTURE V.

On the last occasion I called your attention to important matters appearing on the face of the bill of exchange, and I told you that on this, the next occasion, I should call your attention to important matters appearing on the back of the bill of exchange. But I am bound to tell you that an acceptance may be as well on the back as on the face of the bill, and that which people call an endorsement may be on the face of the instrument. Still, I myself have never seen a bill of exchange in which the acceptance was not on the face of it; I have never seen an indorsement which was not on the back as I now invite you to regard it. Now, before speaking of the transfer and assignment of the debt, which is established by the drawing and acceptance on the face of the instrument, let me for one moment call your attention to the nature of the consideration which must subsist, in order that either the drawer or the indorsee may be said to be a holder for value.

Now the "consideration," we are told, is generally something of some value in the eye of the law; it may be anything that brings profit or advantage or benefit to the promisor, or it may be some detriment or loss which the promisee, at the request of the promisor, incurs, or some responsibility which he undertakes; and you gentlemen practising the law, must make yourselves familiar with the cases which establish what is, and would be in the contemplation of a judge, a consideration for any promise. But I may say to persons who are in business, and who have to deal every day with these instruments, that a bill of exchange or promissory note or cheque, whether given on account of an antecedent debt or in pursuance of a promise made at the time the debt arose, is an instrument given for "consideration" or for value. Now it is important to keep this statement in your minds, because at one time it was supposed that the title of a creditor to a bill of exchange or promissory note, given on account of an antecedent debt, rested upon an implied agreement on his part to suspend his remedies in respect of the debt. If the bill or note were payable at a subsequent date, however short, the creditor would, on this principle, be a holder for value of the bill of exchange or promissory note. It was contended, and in one case was so decided, that where the security given on account of a past debt was a bill of exchange or a promissory note or cheque payable on demand, the person who took it was not a holder for value. It was said that in such case there was no consideration, because the creditor could immediately demand payment of the sum due on the instrument, and did not suspend, nor agree to suspend, his remedies in respect of the antecedent debt. The case to which I have just referred is *Crofts* v. *Beale,* which is reported in 11 Common Bench, p. 172. The defendant was there sought to be made liable, on a promissory note payable on demand, for £400. At the trial it was proved that John Beale was indebted to the plaintiff in the sum of £1,000, and that, being pressed for payment, he and the defendant gave the plaintiff their joint and several note for £400, upon which the action was brought. The jury found there was no agreement to forbear proceedings in respect of the debt of £1,000, or any part thereof, and the Court held that under the circumstances there was no consideration for the promissory note, and the defendant was relieved from all liability. To-day, for reasons to be given, the action would be an undefended one. The same Court, however, in the case of *Belshaw* v. *Bush* (11 Common Bench, p. 191), decided that a bill of exchange given on account of a debt is a conditional payment of the debt, and that until the condition is defeated the bill of exchange operates as an absolute payment of the debt. This principle was applied subsequently in a very important case to bills of exchange and promissory notes payable on demand, and cheques, involving thereby the reversal of the case of *Crofts* v. *Beale*, the particulars of which I have just given you. The case which I submit to you overruled *Crofts* v. *Beale* is the case of *Currie* v. *Misa*, reported in Law Reports, 10 Exchequer, p. 153. I particularly call your attention to the judgment of Mr. Justice Lush, delivering the opinion of the majority of the judges in the Court of Appeal. The other judges who concurred with Justice Lush were Justices Quain, Archibald, and Keating.

In the case of *Currie* v. *Misa* a cheque, payable therefore immediately, was drawn by the defendant Misa on his bankers in favour of Mr. Lizardi or bearer. Lizardi paid the cheque to Glyn, Mills, Currie & Co. on account of a debt which Lizardi owed them. The cheque was not taken for collection. I wish you to note the difference between an instrument taken for collection and an instrument which bankers take on account of a debt due to them. In the latter case, if they take the instrument without suspicion, they are clearly *bonâ fide* holders for value for the full amount. If of course they take a cheque to collect, they may have a lien upon that cheque ; and not only has the banker a lien on the cheque given to him by his customer for collection, but he is deemed, under the provisions of the Act of 1882, section 27, subsection 3, to be a *bonâ fide* holder for value to the extent of his lien ; and therefore it appears that as to every instrument in the possession of a banker upon which he has a lien, if it is a negotiable instrument, he acquires a perfectly good title to it to the extent of his lien against all persons who may claim the bill from him. Either because Lizardi had been guilty of fraud, or there was an entire failure of consideration between himself and the defendant, it was assumed in argument that Lizardi could not maintain any action on the cheque against the defendant. The question then came to be whether the plaintiffs could maintain an action against the defendant by reason of their being *bonâ fide* holders for value. It was admitted they were *bonâ fide* holders, but a great contention arose as to whether they were holders for value, or whether, in other words, they gave consideration to Lizardi for the cheque.

Mr. Justice Lush said that he would not stay to consider whether there was a consideration by way of forbearance for the cheque, although he and his brethren thought there was; and you will see his reference to the authorities and his reasoning in support of that view on pp. 162, 163. Mr. Justice Lush and the majority of the judges decided in favour of the plaintiff on a broader ground than that of whether there was legally any consideration by way of forbearance for the cheque. They held that an existing debt forms of itself a sufficient consideration for a negotiable security payable on demand, so as to constitute the creditor to whom it is given a holder for value. It is scarcely possible to overrate the importance of this judgment to the commercial community. The decision is impaired by the dissenting judgment of the late Lord Coleridge. It is, however, the judgment of four eminent practical lawyers. When the case was before the House of Lords, see 1 App. Cas. p. 554, the Law Lords do not seem to have adopted the simple principle of Mr. Justice Lush, but to have discussed the question whether there was a consideration for the cheque as between Lizardi and Misa. The House of Lords, differing from the assumption of the judges in the Exchequer Chamber, held that there was, and that Lizardi could have sued Misa on the cheque. In that view of the case it became unimportant to consider whether Glyn, Mills & Co. gave

Lizardi consideration for the cheque, although the Law Lords thought they had by the delivery up of a document which Lizardi had drawn upon Misa.

The question, therefore, whether an antecedent debt formed of itself a sufficient consideration for a negotiable security payable on demand remained, even after the decision of the Exchequer Chamber in *Currie v. Misa*, still an open question. It was at length set at rest by section 27, sub-sec. *b* of the Bills of Exchange Act, 1882, by which, in conformity with Mr. Justice Lush's decision, it is enacted that an antecedent debt or liability is deemed a valuable consideration for a bill, whether the bill is payable on demand or at a future time. You will read the section for yourself, because in this part of my course my lectures are only an introduction I hope to your complete mastery and study of this Act of 1882, my object being simply to facilitate your study of all its various clauses. The provision I have stated relating to a bill of exchange applies to a promissory note and to a cheque. It is therefore clear law now, that a person who takes *bonâ fide* and for a past debt a negotiable instrument payable on demand acquires a title to it independent of the question of forbearance. So much for the question of consideration; but you must keep it in mind, because if a man draws a bill upon an acceptor, and there is no consideration for the drawing, and the name is lent for the accommodation of the drawer, no action will lie by the drawer against the acceptor; and if the drawer should pass it to another person without value, such person cannot sue the acceptor. But remember, if you are pleading to an action on a bill against the acceptor, you must allege failure of consideration between the acceptor and drawer, and failure of consideration between the drawer and the holder; and remember this, too, that in consequence of the presumption that every dealing with a bill is for value, the burthen of proving these allegations and each of them, rests upon the defendant who pleads them.

Let me now pass to the transfer of a bill; and here I may say that I find a phrase that I do not much like in the Act of 1882, sect. 31 (1). It says: "A bill is negotiated when it is transferred from one person to another in such a manner as to constitute the transferee the holder of the bill." I prefer these simple words: "A bill may be transferred"—that is all you want to learn —"from one person to another in such a manner as to constitute the transferee the holder of the bill." In the expression "negotiated when it is transferred" the framers of the Act are not using the word "negotiated" there in the sense in which I use the word "negotiable"; all that they mean by the expression is, you may transfer a bill of exchange from one person to another so as to constitute the transferee the holder of the bill. So you may.

Now, just let us see for a moment how it is done; and if you will take into your hands the * lithographed form No. 10, which I have had prepared for you, I will make such observations as the various indorsements seem to call for. Those of you who kept the specimen bills Nos. 1 to 9 of last week will please refer to No. 2. You will find there that William Smith is the drawer of the bill. How, then, can William Smith transfer the property in that bill? As it is payable to his order he can only do it by putting his name on the back of the instrument and delivering it *with the intention of passing the property therein.* I should like to add these last words to the definition of sect. 31 of the Act of 1882 :— The Legislature there says, "A bill payable to bearer is negotiated by delivery." "A bill payable to order is negotiated by the endorsement of the holder completed by delivery." The delivery in each case must be with the intention of passing the property

* *The two forms used at this lecture will be found on the pages prior to this lecture.*

therein. Therefore, if William Smith indorses his name upon the bill and says to his clerk, "Take this into the next room and make a copy of it," the property in the instrument has not passed to the clerk, although it has been delivered into his hands. There has not been a delivery within the meaning of this section or within the principles of our law: "delivery" in the section means delivery with the intention of passing the property in the bill. If the clerk should, however, without authority pass the bill to a *bonâ fide* holder for value, William Smith would be liable to him as an indorser. *Marston* v. *Allen*, 8 Meeson and Welsby, p. 494.

Let me assume now that you are looking at the form No. 10, and regarding it as if it were the back of No. 2. The first thing you see on it is the signature of "William Smith" simply. Then he must also have delivered it, as, so far as he is concerned, the property will not pass by his act unless he not only writes his name but delivers the instrument. Now let me tell you, in dealing with matters arising out of bills of exchange, you must know and discuss the principles of almost every department of law. You must learn, therefore, the law of principal and agent. I cannot discuss the law of principal and agent in my six lectures, but I may say that delivery to an agent will be delivery to the principal. It is important also to remember that you are now dealing not so much with contract as with conveyance and transfer in this part of our study. There is no contract made between the person to whom William Smith delivered the bill and the acceptor, by reason merely of the delivery. The indorsee may, however, by the law merchant sue the acceptor upon the contract he has entered into with the drawer, although the indorsee was not a party originally to that contract. There may be two or three contracts between William Smith and James Robinson, and a contract, of course, by his accepting. There might have been a contract before his accepting by his having promised to accept, but in dealing with indorsement we are dealing with a case of transfer and conveyance. Now remember this elementary principle, that as to a contract you must have the consent of two or more parties to make it. A conveyance is operative without the consent at all of the person in whose favour it is made. Do not forget that. It is a principle that is applicable in many departments of our law. Let me show you its applicability to bills of exchange by referring you to the case of *Lysaght* v. *Bryant*, which you will find reported in 9 Common Bench, p. 46. That was a case in which Lysaght and another were in partnership. They had in their possession a bill drawn by the defendant upon a man named Matthews. Lysaght and his partner were indebted to the father of Lysaght in a large sum of money. They were in difficulties. They wished to reduce the debt which they owed to Lysaght senior, and evidence was given (and the jury found it to be true) that one day Lysaght and his partner agreed that the bill which they had received from the defendant should be transferred to the father of Lysaght in reduction of his debt. They accordingly endorsed the bill to Lysaght the father, and the son of the plaintiff, with the consent of his partner, put it into the cash-box, and held it for the use of Lysaght the father, who sued as plaintiff. What did the Court hold? That although the plaintiff knew nothing about the transaction at the time it took place, yet, being a case of conveyance and transfer, the property in the bill passed to Lysaght the father immediately that transaction took place, and that until he disclaimed the property, he continued the owner of the bill. You must study the word "delivery" and the meaning of the word "possession." The Court held that, upon the facts found by the jury, there had been an indorsement and delivery by the firm to the son as the father's agent, and that the possession of the son was the possession of the father. The transaction was the same as if the father had been present at the time of the indorsement, and received the bill.

When "Mr. William Smith" has put his name on the back of the bill in the way you see, and delivered it with the intention of passing the property therein, the bill now can be transferred by simple delivery. Remember, these are things that you are to have present to your mind at a glance. I am talking about things that must be in your minds ready for use at any moment —not to be ascertained by looking into a Bills of Exchange Act. Now the moment "William Smith" has put the bill into that state, it can now be transferred by delivery. Therefore the person to whom "William Smith" gives it can pass it by delivery at once, without any writing on the back of the bill, and his transferee will have a perfectly good title. It may go, perhaps, through three hands by simple delivery, and at length it gets into the hands of Mr. James Richardson. Now let me tell you—it is important that you should remember this—that no person can be sued on a bill of exchange who does not put his name to it. If, of course, a man has given you a bill of exchange, promising to put his name to it and intending to do so, if he does not on request put his name to it, you can take proceedings to compel him to do so, but not unless he intended to do it, and it was so understood. If he does not put his name, you simply have a title to the bill but no claim thereon against the transferor. Therefore, if you want any person's responsibility on the bill, you must get him to put his name on the back of the bill; but if he does not you cannot sue him on the bill. He is not, however, free from all responsibility and obligation; far from it. A man who transfers a bill to another for value, although he does not put his name on the instrument, warrants his transferee that there is no defect in the instrument; that the bill is what it purports to be; that he himself has a perfect right to transfer it, and he himself is not aware of anything which would render it valueless. If you want authority on this point, you will find it, apart from the Bills of Exchange Act, 1882, sect. 58, in the case of *Gurney* v. *Womersley,* which is reported in 4 Ellis & Blackburn, p. 133. Womersley was a broker in the City. Overend, Gurney & Co. took a bill from the defendant to be discounted by them, but it did not have Womersley's name upon it. As a rule, bill brokers who offer bills for discount do not put their names on the bills they offer. It turned out that the acceptance was a forgery, and that the supposed drawer and first indorser were fictitious persons. The bill, in short, was worthless. The Court held that Gurneys could get back the money which they paid as upon a failure of consideration, and sue, as in former days we used to do, for money had and received, as money which the defendant was bound to return. Now, when you hear, as I have often heard people say in a hasty way: " Oh, you cannot sue him, his name is not on the bill," please remember there are obligations which exist outside the bill, and although his name be not upon the bill, the person who transfers it to you does incur obligations, and obligations to the extent I have mentioned.

Now look again at the specimen. I will assume that this bill has come through two or three hands if you like, and at last it has reached the hands of Mr. James Richardson. What does Mr. James Richardson do when he parts with the bill? He writes over his name, " Pay Thomas Daft." It does not matter whether there is " or order " or not; there is no difference between " Thomas Daft " and " Thomas Daft or order." Richardson writes, " Pay Thomas Daft, James Richardson." " William Smith's " indorsement is what is called a " blank " indorsement. Now you have " James Richardson's " indorsement, and his is a special indorsement, and an indorsement to pay " Thomas Daft." When it is in that form, Thomas Daft cannot part with the property in this instrument according to mercantile law by mere delivery, although there have been intermediate dealings with the bill by delivery, and although William Smith made it a bill transferable by delivery. Now again, by Richardson's indorsement, it has become a specially indorsed bill, and Thomas Daft must put his name to it in order to transfer the property therein, just as William Smith was obliged to put his name on the back because the bill was drawn to his order. Now I put the following indorsements before you because some people have asked me: "Do you mean you can have two or three blank indorsements?" Certainly, one after the other, and here they come. Thomas Daft desires to pass the property in the bill, and he does so by indorsement and delivery. Thomas Daft indorses in blank; "William Hartley," to whom Daft delivered it, indorses in blank; and "Mark Phillips," to whom Hartley delivered it, indorses it in blank. There you see three blank indorsements one after the other. That of Thomas Daft was necessary in order to transfer the property in the bill. William Hartley and Mark Phillips could each of them have transferred the property in the bill without indorsement, but their names were put on the bill in order to make them liable on it. When the bill has been indorsed in blank it is not essential, in order to transfer the property, that the transferor should put his name on the bill, but it is necessary he should do so if you desire to make him a party to the bill and that he should incur to you the obligations of indorser of the instrument. You can thus have several indorsers in blank; I have put them on the form because I have seen as many as these in my time. Now the bill comes into the hands of Mr. George French, who says, "Pay James Saunders," and therefore you have again the bill which has been indorsed in blank two or three times before, an instrument again specially indorsed; and, if you are going to deal with "James Saunders," you must have "James Saunders's" signature in order to a valid transfer of the bill.

I may tell you practical lawyers, who may have to do with bills of exchange in Court, that if ever you should be suing, say, in the name of "George French," and you are suing, perhaps, "William Smith," the drawer, and you have a difficulty in proving all these various endorsements and transfers which are upon this bill, you may strike out the intervening endorsements, and allege it to be a transfer by William Smith to George French. Of course, if you strike out the intervening names of the parties to the instrument you lose, if I remember rightly, your remedy against them; but, subject to that, you can at once, if you are in a difficulty in Court (and I hope you will be in some cases soon, to show your skill in getting out of apparent difficulties), say: "Very well, my lord, I will strike out all these indorsements. I will take the first indorsement that is in blank, 'William Smith;' that will do for me." Then prove his signature, and that you are the holder for value, and your case is complete.

Now, the next matter I desire to place before you is this. Never forget that a man may be a party to a bill of exchange in two or three capacities. An acceptor may become first of all an indorsee; then in his turn he may become an indorser. So may a man who has drawn the bill, after five or six dealings with the instrument, become an indorsee, and again may become indorser; and so, with every one of the indorsers in the same way, each one may become indorsee and again an indorser. But only, mind you, with this consequence: that if the acceptor becomes an indorsee, he cannot charge any antecedent party to the bill, who would have a remedy over against him upon the bill as acceptor. I hope you follow me. I tell you the acceptor may become indorsee, and may become indorser, exactly as if his name had never been on the instrument, but only with this condition: that the acceptor who becomes an indorsee—(and very naturally you can see the reason, viz. to prevent circuity of action)—can never maintain an action against any of the prior parties to the bill if those prior parties could maintain an action against him upon the instrument. If they could not, then he is entitled still to sue. The same with the drawer, the same with the indorser; and therefore I have, on purpose to show you this, given you the name of James Robinson as an indorser, and I have put against his name the word, in brackets, "acceptor." You will find, therefore, that the acceptor may still become an indorsee, and may also become an indorser, of course, subject to the rules which I have just mentioned as to his right over against the prior parties to the instrument.

Now I want to call your attention to a matter which is sometimes overlooked. A man may write the name of an indorsee on a bill of exchange, and yet not be liable himself upon the instrument. Now, you will notice that James Robinson has specially indorsed the bill: "Pay William Robertson; James Robinson." Assume that William Robertson indorses the bill in blank: it is now in order again for the property passing by delivery; but you also see over the name "William Robertson," the direction "Pay Jonathan George." That direction, "Pay Jonathan George," may not have been written by William Robertson at all. That may have been written by a man to whom the bill has been transferred after it has been passed two or three times by delivery to different people, not one of whom has put his name to the bill. Then a person who does not want to put his name to the bill may desire to state on the face of the bill to whom the property in it shall go, and he does so by writing "Pay Jonathan George" over the simple blank indorsement of "William Robertson." Do I make myself understood? William Robertson has put his name simply. It is then transferable by delivery; it can pass by delivery. Suppose William Robertson gave it to

James Gladstone, and James Gladstone, without putting his name on it, gave it to Richard Cobden, and Richard Cobden desires to pass the property in the bill to Jonathan George, he may do so by writing "Jonathan George" over the signature of William Robertson, and handing it to Jonathan George. Richard Cobden has thus, without rendering himself liable on the instrument, turned the indorsement of "William Robertson" into a special indorsement, and Jonathan George in his turn must indorse the instrument in order to pass the property therein.

Now, if you will just keep these things in your minds, you will not have much trouble in dealing with the indorsements that appear on the back of the bill, and which are the means, together with delivery, by which the property in the bill is, and can be, transferred. You must clearly distinguish between an "indorsement in blank," and a "special indorsement." You must remember that you can have an indorsement in blank followed by a special indorsement; then you know the conditions under which in each case the property may be passed. Then you may have an indorsement in blank again, followed by another special indorsement; and then ultimately you may have a person turning a blank indorsement, not his own, into a special indorsement by putting over the blank indorsement the name of his transferee, although he himself has not put his name to the bill and cannot be sued upon it.

There are one or two things more that I want to say to you in reference to the transfer of bills of exchange. Under the Act of 1882 it is established beyond all doubt that if a bill is indorsed conditionally, the acceptor may disregard the condition, and payment by him to the indorsee is valid although the condition has not been performed. So that now if you were to have a conditional indorsement thus: "Pay A. B. or order on his handing over to me certain bills of lading, Thomas Johnson," the acceptor may pay the value to the lawful holder of the bill, although there is this condition upon it, and the acceptor need not trouble himself whether the condition has been fulfilled. What the responsibility is between the person who takes the instrument conditionally and the person who transfers it, at present we need not stay to discuss. There would be no doubt whatever that he would be bound by that condition and have to answer for any improper dealing with the instrument contrary to the express agreement between the parties.

Now there is another thing I want to tell you. You cannot have a partial indorsement. You can have a partial acceptance. You cannot say, "Pay A. B. £50 of the within £100." That is no indorsement at all; whether conditional or not, the indorsement must be for the entire amount of the bill. If nothing is said on the bill, the indorsement will be presumed to be for the entire bill. Further, let me tell you that if the instrument has been indorsed or made payable to the order of two or more persons severally, they must all put their names to the instrument in order to transfer it unless one is appointed to act for the others, or the persons named stand in the relation of partners. Then you can have what are called "restrictive indorsements," and such indorsements put an end, apparently, to the transferability of the bill in the ordinary sense of that word. Here are one or two illustrations. "Pay D. or order for collection;" "Pay D. only." Those are what are called "restrictive indorsements," and there is by them no transfer of the ownership in the bill. D. has, however, a right to receive payment of the bill and to sue any person his indorser could have sued.

The next thing I want to speak to you about is an overdue bill of exchange. Of course you know what I mean by "overdue." Assuming a bill was drawn on the 1st January at three months, it would be payable on the 4th April, and if not paid on that day, the instrument would be said to be overdue and "dishonoured." If, then, it comes into your hands after such dishonour, it would be said to come into your hands "disgraced." A bill of exchange payable on demand may be disgraced by mere lapse of time. By the Act of 1882, a bill payable on demand is overdue when it appears on the face of it to have been in circulation for an unreasonable time. What is an unreasonable length of time is a question of fact. It is otherwise with a promissory note. If a promissory note, payable on demand, has been negotiated, it is not to be deemed overdue for the purpose of affecting the holder with defects of title, of which he had no notice, by reason that a reasonable time for presenting it for payment has elapsed since its issue. If the instrument is disgraced, you cannot have a better title than the man had, who transferred it to you.

Then just let us see in what position does the transferee of a bill of exchange stand who takes it overdue and disgraced? First of all I may say this (and I believe really it will cover all the cases), that the person takes the instrument subject to all the equities (mark the word) arising out of the original transaction. If there has been fraud or duress, of course it is clear that you take it subject to the defence which those matters afford, and you can have no better title than the person who transferred it to you; but, further than that, you take it subject to the equities arising out of the original transaction. These words, "the equities arising out of the original transaction," must be carefully considered. A., the holder of a disgraced bill of exchange, indorses it to B. If A. sued the acceptor, the acceptor would have a set-off equal to the amount of the bill. Would B. be affected by that set-off in an action against A.? No; the set-off does not arise out of the original transaction. B. would not be affected by the set-off even if he knew of it at the time he took the bill, and took it for the purpose of defeating the acceptor's set-off. You will best understand the words "equities arising out of the transaction," by studying a case which I trust you will endeavour to keep in your mind.

Read the case of *Holmes* v. *Kidd*, reported in the 3rd Hurlstone & Norman, p. 891. This case which I am going to give you was not a case of fraud, duress, or illegality of any kind, and yet the person who took the bill in that case when it was disgraced, was met for the larger portion of the bill with an absolutely good defence. Now, just follow me. In the case of *Holmes* v. *Kidd*, Kidd, the acceptor, wanted some money, and he went to a man and asked him if he would lend him £300. "Yes," said the man, "I will lend you £300; give me your acceptance for the £300 at three months, and lodge with me goods, so that, if you do not pay the bill, I may sell the goods and pay myself out of the proceeds." Kidd agreed to these terms. The bill was accepted, the goods were deposited, and the money lent; the bill was dishonoured. The goods were sold by the drawer, and £272 was realised and received by him. Then the drawer, acting dishonourably, passed the bill to the plaintiff in the action. To the declaration in the action the defendant pleaded thus: When I accepted this bill, I accepted it upon a condition that the right to sue me on the bill by the drawer should be defeasible by his exercising a power of selling the goods which I gave him as a security for the instrument, and the promise that he would deduct from the amount of the bill the amount realised by the sale of the goods. The drawer, on my not meeting the bill, sold the goods, and realised £272 thereby, and then indorsed the bill to the plaintiff. This defence does not involve a question of notice at all; it has nothing to do with notice. The plaintiff took the bill after it was dishonoured. Held, by the Court of Exchequer Chamber to be a perfectly good defence to the extent of £272, and upon this short ground, that it was not a question of notice on the part of the plaintiff, or want of good faith on the part of the plaintiff, but that as he was the transferee of the bill after it was dishonoured, he took it subject to all the equities arising out of the original transaction. You see, this is not a case of set-off which exists outside the transaction of the bill altogether, and is merely personal to the holder; but this is a case in which, when the very bill was conceived and created, the right under it was to be defeasible upon the realization of the goods; and so the Court held in that case, that the person who took it, although it may have been taken *bonâ fide*, as he took it disgraced, had no title to the instrument, except to the extent of £28.

Now there is one other matter which I think I can deal with perhaps satisfactorily to-night in the time which is now remaining to me, and that is as to the question upon whom the burden of proof rests, as to consideration and *bona fides*, where there has been fraud, illegality of consideration, or duress in respect of the bill, or the bill has been stolen, or there has been an improper dealing with it. You understand of course what "duress" means. It is making a man put his name to a bill by a threat of force, as if the drawer should say, for example, "If you do not put your name to this bill as acceptor before you leave this room, I will do you some bodily harm." You understand of course what "illegality of consideration" means. I cannot stay to discuss with you to-night the many rules at common law and the various statutes which make certain considerations illegal; you yourselves must study " illegality of consideration " as part of the general law. As to a case of fraud, you know generally that it exists wherever a person represents some fact as existing which does not exist, the person making the representation knowing it to be untrue, or not caring whether it is true or false. Now do not think that those are the only cases which give rise to the question of the burden of proof. Any improper dealing with the bill by the person who transfers it will raise the question of the burden of proof; and the case I always keep in my mind on this point is the case of *Hall v. Featherstone*, which is reported in 3 Hurlstone & Norman, p. 284. That is the case of one man saying to another: "I am pressed for money. Can you help me?" The answer is: "I will easily get some money for you by discounting your acceptance. How much would you like?" "£65." "Very well; give me your acceptance: I will put my name to it as drawer, and then I will go and get it discounted and send or bring you the money." It frequently happens that a gentleman of this description, as soon as he gets the bill, parts with it immediately perhaps for some debt of his own, or for some few sovereigns given to him to live upon for the next few days, or to indulge whatever tastes or habits may be most pleasant to himself. In *Hall v. Featherstone*, the acceptor was left entirely in the lurch. Read that case, and although in it there was no fraud in procuring the acceptance, no duress, no illegality of consideration, yet the man who transferred the bill to the holder dealt with the bill in a manner that was dishonest and improper. The Court held, that such a state of things called for proof on the part of the holder of the bill, the extent of which I will mention directly.

Now what is the burthen of proof which under such circumstances is cast upon the claimant who alleges he is a *bonâ fide* holder for value? As to that the Court of Appeal have decided, in a case in which I was engaged (but not reported), that as soon as ever a defendant in an action upon a bill establishes fraud, duress, illegality of consideration, or improper dealing with the instrument, the man who seeks to recover upon the bill must establish to the satisfaction of the Court or jury not only that he is a holder for value, but that he is an *honest* holder for value. The great question in dispute was, and had been for many years, whether all that he was called upon to do was to show consideration, leaving the defendant to establish that the plaintiff took it dishonestly. But, say the Courts now (and I think the words of the Act of 1882 are sufficiently strong to support their decision), "You, the plaintiff, must, now that evidence of fraud has been given, if you want to recover upon the bill, not only show that you gave value for it, but you must satisfy the tribunal that you took the bill honestly." I need scarcely say there is a difference, and a very great difference, between the defendant showing that the plaintiff took it dishonestly and the plaintiff showing that he took it honestly. The burden of proof of both honesty and value rests upon the plaintiff. I tell you that the moment the defendant has given evidence from which the jury may properly infer that the bill was obtained by fraud, or by duress, or that there was illegality of consideration, or any improper dealing with the bill, the defendant is no longer called upon to sustain the further allegations contained in his plea, that the plaintiff took it without value and with notice. The burden is at once shifted, and the plaintiff must show that he took it for value, and that he took it honestly. See the difference. The plaintiff will have to be put in the box. If he is not called, or his absence accounted for, although he may give evidence of the consideration for the bill by a person who was present at the transaction, the jury will not find that he took the instrument honestly. It very often happens at the close of the cross-examination of the plaintiff, the inadequacy of the consideration and other circumstances disclosed therein, establish the fact that he took it dishonestly. Mark you, do not forget that word "consideration." The consideration given very often is conclusive, as I have told you, upon the question of *bona fides*. If I found that the plaintiff gave half the value for good commercial bills that could be discounted at 5 per cent. per annum in the City

—bills that had been accepted in the name of the firm by a partner for gambling transactions in fraud of the partnership—I should soon come to the conclusion that the plaintiff did not take them honestly, because he could not have believed that the man was parting with bills that he came by honestly, and which were his property, at half their value. Therefore, always work your cases like this: If the plaintiff has given a small consideration, show the extreme value of the instrument and what the transferor could have got if it had been discounted properly. Hence, with respect to a Bank of England note, if a man gave three pounds for a £5 Bank of England note there is not one of you, unless there were some very extraordinary circumstances, who would hesitate for a moment to find that the man who took the note for three pounds, for which an honest man anywhere could get £5, must have suspected that the person parting with the note, or some person for whom he was acting, had come by the note dishonestly. This is an illustration I have heard used by great judges in order to explain to a jury how the inadequacy of consideration should affect their minds in dealing with the question of *bona fides*. As a rule, honest people want full or fair value for the property they are parting with. So much for this part of the case. If there has been improper dealing with the bill, fraud, or duress, then the person who sues must show that he is a holder for value, and that he took the bill honestly. If, of course, he did take the bill honestly, although carelessly, negligently, although he took it in a way that perhaps no twelve rational men would have taken the instrument, although he took it for inadequate consideration, yet if you come to the conclusion that he did take it *bonâ fide* and for value, he is perfectly entitled to recover upon the bill.

Now, I am sure you will remember that in delivering these six lectures how much I have to compress, and with what haste I am obliged to advance. Therefore, if you will bear with me I think I can just deal to-night with one more matter, and that is presentment of a bill of exchange for acceptance. Now, if you will look at specimen No. 1 of the bills, I told you that was a perfect bill of exchange because there are drawer and drawee, although no acceptor. The drawer of such a bill may part with the property in it before it is accepted. Now, what you have to learn is, when the holder of a bill of exchange is bound to present the instrument for acceptance. He must do so when the bill is payable after sight, in order to fix the maturity of the instrument. He must do so if the bill expressly stipulates that it shall be presented for acceptance. He must also present the bill for acceptance where it is drawn, payable elsewhere than at the residence or place of business of the drawee. It must be presented for acceptance before it can be presented for payment. If the holder of a bill drawn payable elsewhere than at the residence or place of business of the drawee has not time, using reasonable care, to present the bill for acceptance before presenting it for payment on the day it falls due, the delay in presenting the bill for acceptance is excused. When a bill payable after sight is transferred, the holder must either present it for acceptance or part with it within a reasonable time. If you will look at specimen No. 1, you will see it is addressed to James Robinson, at 52, Old Change, London. There is nothing to show that the bill is drawn payable elsewhere than the place of business or residence of Mr. Robinson; it need not be presented for acceptance. If it is drawn as appears on the second page of the forms inserted prior to this lecture, and marked No. 11, it must be presented for acceptance. The address of the drawee is at 52, Old Change, and the bill is drawn payable at Barclay, Bevan & Co., Lombard Street. The bill in that case must be presented for acceptance.

The holder of bill No. 1 may present the bill for acceptance prior to the day of payment if he chooses, but is not obliged to do so. If the drawee refuses to accept the bill, the holder must give notice of such refusal to all prior parties on the bill except the drawee, and may sue them upon the bill as being dishonoured by non-acceptance, no presentment for payment being necessary. Apart from a contract, neither the holder of the bill nor any other party to the bill has an action against the drawee for not accepting.

The presentment for acceptance must be made, by or on behalf of the holder, to the drawee at a reasonable hour on a business day, and before the bill is overdue. If there are two or more drawees who are not partners, presentment for acceptance must be made to all, unless one has authority to act for all, and then the presentment may be made to him only. It is not necessary in all cases to take the instrument to the residence of the drawee, or his place of business; it may be presented for acceptance through the post, when the post office may be used pursuant to agreement or usage. Where the drawee is dead, then the bill may be presented to his personal representatives; if bankrupt, then to his trustee. Where, however, the drawee is dead or bankrupt, presentment for acceptance is excused, and the bill may be regarded as dishonoured by non-acceptance. It is also excused if, after using all reasonable care, presentment cannot be effected. I told you the other day that there may be a qualified or conditional acceptance of a bill of exchange. The holder of the bill may take such conditional acceptance if he likes. He may, however, refuse to do so; and if he cannot get an unqualified acceptance he may treat the bill as dishonoured by non-acceptance.

I will proceed in my next lecture to discuss presentment of a bill of exchange for payment, and the rules relating to notice of dishonour, and deal shortly with promissory notes and cheques. As the next lecture will be the last, perhaps you will grant me a longer allowance than an hour, in order to present in six lectures an outline—I am afraid a bare and imperfect outline—of this important department of our law.

No. 12.

London, *September 1st, 1895.*

£100 : 0 : 0.

At sight
On demand

Three months after date I promise to pay to James Johnson, or {Bearer} {Order}, the sum of One Hundred Pounds.

ROBERT GODFREY.

No. 13.

LONDON, *September 1st, 1895.*

Three months after date I promise to pay to my own Order the sum of One Hundred Pounds.

£100 : 0 : 0.

ROBERT GODFREY.

LECTURE VI.

I HAVE been fully occupied since I last had the honour of speaking to you, and have not had much time for reflection on the law of negotiable securities. But I propose this evening, in my last address, to run quickly through the subjects which still await our consideration—viz., the presentation of the bill for payment, and the notice of dishonour that must be given if the holder wishes to charge the drawer and indorsers of the bill; then to say a few words upon promissory notes; speak of cheques and the relation of banker and customer; call your attention to one or two cases with respect to crossed cheques; explain the effect of the principal provisions as to crossed cheques in the Act of 1882, which are only re-enactments of earlier statutes, and then to say farewell.

Now, in order to charge the drawer or indorsers, the bill must be duly presented for payment. That would be done by any person taking the instrument, going to a certain defined place, which I will mention directly, and asking for payment. He should shew the bill to the person from whom he demands payment, and if the bill be paid he should deliver it up to the person paying it. If there is no person there, either the acceptor or his agent, of course there is no use in making any request, and you are not bound to do so; and if you have exercised reasonable diligence to find the acceptor or to find his agent, after the exercise of that reasonable diligence, you are not called upon to take any further steps. But to charge the drawer and indorser the step of presentment must be taken, except in some few cases. Now the bill must be presented on the day it falls due. That is, if the bill is drawn three months from the 1st of January, it must be presented (because you know there are the days of grace) on the 4th of April; and on that day it must be presented, unless there are certain circumstances to which I shall call your attention. If the bill is payable on demand, you have a great difficulty in determining when and under what circumstances presentation for payment should take place. You cannot be relieved from the obligation of exercising your own judgment as to when such a bill should be presented. It has been enacted, that in the case of a bill payable on demand, in order to charge the drawer, presentment for payment must be made within a reasonable time after its issue; and to charge the indorser it must be presented within a reasonable time after its indorsement.

Now, in determining what is a reasonable time for the presentation of a bill payable on demand, both men of business and lawyers have a difficult task. There is no certain rule for their guidance. They are told that in determining what is a reasonable time for presentment, regard is to be had to the nature of the bill, the usage of trade with regard to similar bills, and the facts of the particular case, all which practically means this, you have no other guidance really but your own good sense and your acquaintance with business usages. This same direction is given in the case of a promissory note in order to charge the indorser, and I can only advise you, that if you are the indorsee of a promissory note or bill of exchange payable on demand, to present it for payment at once, and if any considerable time has elapsed since its issue, or indorsement, decline to discount or cash it unless you can rely on the solvency of the maker of the note, or acceptor of the bill of exchange. These are the considerations with respect to the presentment for payment of an instrument payable on demand. I have told you, that in some cases you must present the bill for acceptance. Where it has not been accepted, and is drawn payable at sight, in order to get the date from which the bill is to run, you must present the bill for acceptance. If acceptance has been refused, and notice has been given of non-acceptance to the drawer or indorsers, a cause of action accrues against them at once, and unless the bill is accepted in the meantime you need not present the bill again for payment, if the acceptance of it has been refused. In all matters, therefore, of presentment for payment, you have only to bear in mind that a bill payable on demand will require most careful consideration by you of all the circumstances before you can decide that an action will lie against the drawer or indorser; and in the case of a man of business, the fewer he takes of outstanding promissory notes, or bills payable on demand, the better. Now, a bill must be presented by the holder or some person authorised to receive payment on his behalf. The bill must be presented for payment on a business day, and at a reasonable hour; you must go to the place where the bill is payable in reasonable hours. Now, let us consider the place where you are to go to. Always bear in mind the person of whom you are speaking. When you are talking of an acceptor, please never allow the thought of an indorser to enter your mind; keep to the acceptor. With respect to the acceptor, I have told you that except in one instance, you are not called upon to present the bill in order to charge him at all; so far as the acceptor is concerned, there is no occasion to protest the bill in case he does not meet the bill, nor is the holder called upon to give him notice of dishonour; unless you have a qualified acceptance as to place, you need not trouble yourself with presentation in order to charge the acceptor. In the case of a qualified acceptance as to place, the bill must be presented for payment in order to charge the acceptor. It is not necessary, however, to present the bill for payment on the day it matures. If the acceptance is conditional, for example, on giving up certain bills of lading, it is not necessary, in order to charge the acceptor, to present the bill for payment and tender the bills of lading on the day the bill matures. The bills of lading must, however, be tendered to the acceptor before he can be made liable on the bill. The acceptor may, if he likes, make his acceptance conditional on the bills being given up to him on the day his acceptance becomes due, and if the bills of lading are not so tendered to him he will be discharged from all liability on the bill (*Smith* v. *Virtue*, 9 Common Bench, New Series, p. 214). But to charge the drawer, and to charge every person whose name is on the back of the bill, you must present the bill for payment on the day it matures, and you must present the bill at the place where it is accepted payable; therefore if it is accepted payable at Barclay, Bevan & Co., as I have told you, you must present it there—*à fortiori*, if it is accepted "not elsewhere and not otherwise."

Now, the next thing to remember is this: that if there is no place mentioned in the acceptance, then you will look to see if the address of the acceptor is on the bill. If so, you must take it there, and present it to him for payment. If there is no address on the bill, then find out the place of business of the acceptor, or if you cannot find out that, then find out his place of residence. Present it at either of those places and the presentation for payment will be good. If you do not know the acceptor's place of business or private address, then you can present it to the acceptor wherever you can find him, or at his last known place of business or residence. You must keep these things in your minds; they are not to be merely in your notebooks, or to be found in your "Byles on Bills," but they must be in your minds ready for use at a moment's notice. If you present the bill according to these rules and no one authorised to pay or refuse payment can be found there, you need not trouble yourself with any further presentment.

If the bill is accepted by two or more persons who are not partners, and no place of payment is specified, you must present it to each one of them in order to charge the drawer and indorsers. I need scarcely tell you that if you cannot present the bill for payment through circumstances over which you have no control, and the circumstances are not due to your default, then the delay in presentment will be excused. But the moment that those circumstances causing the delay have ceased to exist, then due diligence must begin at once to be exercised. When the cause of the delay ceases, then I tell you that presentment must take place with reasonable diligence. Presentment of course is excused also when you have endeavoured to find out the acceptor in the way I have mentioned to you, and you are unable to do so. If you cannot find his business address, and cannot find his place of residence, or meet with the acceptor himself, then presentation for payment will be excused. Now I must guard you against a rather common error. I have known the error I am going to mention to you committed several times in my own experience. The error is in supposing you are excused from presenting a bill for payment, because you have every reason to believe that the bill will be dishonoured if you do present it. Such a belief, although rightly grounded, will not excuse presentment. You must go and present the bill to the acceptor even although you think he will not pay the bill. You are not excused because you believe that your journey will be fruitless.

In the case of a fictitious drawee, there is no occasion to present the bill for payment, and in the case of an acceptance for the accommodation of the drawer you need not present it for payment to charge the drawer ; and if you look at the case of *Bickerdike* v. *Bollman*, which is in the second volume of Smith's Leading Cases, p. 99 (10th edit.), you will find the reasons given for the principle which has just been enunciated and the cases in which notice of dishonour need not be given. It really would be best, some have thought, to have a fixed rule that the drawer should receive notice of dishonour in all cases. A bill of exchange, it is said, supposes that the drawer has funds in the hands of the acceptor in respect of which he is drawing, and that he is entitled to have the earliest intimation of the failure of his acceptor to pay, in order that he may withdraw those funds, if possible, at the earliest moment. The reason for this obligation to give the drawer notice of dishonour cannot apply to the case of an acceptance for the accommodation of the drawer. The drawer has no money in the hands of the acceptor, nor belief that the acceptor will have any. There is no money to withdraw, and no injury will be done to the drawer by not informing him of the dishonour.

Therefore the Courts have held that with respect to the drawer of an accommodation bill, a bill as to which there is no reason at all to believe that the acceptor will be in funds, you need not give the drawer notice of dishonour. The case of *Bickerdike* v. *Bollman* will render you familiar with the reasons for the rule that in the case of an accommodation acceptance, notice of dishonour need not be given to the drawer. The Act of 1882, clause (c) of section 46, puts the law thus: Presentment for payment is dispensed with as regards the drawer where the drawee or acceptor is not bound as between himself and the drawer to accept or pay the bill, and the drawer has no reason to believe that the bill would be paid if presented.

Now comes another and important matter which you will have to consider, and that is how far are you obliged to give notice of dishonour to an indorser who has indorsed the instrument for the accommodation of one of the prior parties? If you will look at the case of *Carter* v. *Flowers*, the case I always keep in my mind, reported in 16 Meeson & Welsby,

p. 743, you will see the discussion there as to when an accommodation indorser is entitled to notice of dishonour; and it is clear that if he has accepted for the accommodation of one of the prior parties he would on payment have a right to recover over against such party, and I think in such case would be entitled to notice of dishonour. The lawyer should remember that the indorser in certain circumstances is not entitled to notice of dishonour and presentment for payment, so far as he is concerned, is dispensed with. When the instrument has been accepted and drawn for the accommodation of the indorser, and he has no reason to expect that the bill would be paid if presented, he is not entitled to notice of dishonour. Therefore, if you get an accommodation acceptance, which means that the acceptor has had no value, and also find that the drawer has received no value, but the bill has been drawn and accepted for the benefit of the indorser, then, under the recent code, you need not present the bill for payment in order to charge the indorser if he has no reason to believe that the bill will be paid if presented. I would say to men of business, however, do not stay to discuss these distinctions, but give notice of dishonour, if possible, to the drawer and every indorser of the bill. The lawyer should remember these refinements in order to be able to help you by his learning in case you should fail to give the ordinary notice of dishonour.

Now, subject to the rules I have told you, if the bill be not presented for payment the drawer and indorser are discharged. But even if the bill has been presented for payment and is dishonoured something more remains to be done in order to charge the drawer and indorser. Notice of dishonour of the bill must be given by the holder to all prior parties to the bill (except of course the acceptor) in order to charge them all. He may, if he thinks fit, give notice to only one or two if he thinks they are well able to pay the bill. The indorser who has received notice of dishonour should himself give notice of dishonour to all the previous indorsers and the drawer, lest the holder should not have done so. Now, notice of dishonour may be given by or on behalf of the holder or by or on behalf of an indorser who at the time of giving it is liable on the bill, or it may be given of course by an agent acting for his principal, either in his own name or in the name of any party entitled to give notice. If it is given by the holder, who can avail himself of notice of dishonour given by the holder? The holder of course himself, and all the subsequent holders of the bill. I have told you that the fact of the bill being dishonoured, does not prevent its being transferred from one man to another; it passes subject to the equities as I told you in one of my previous lectures. But the notice of dishonour that has been given by the holder will avail for all the persons to whom the instrument may be subsequently indorsed. Is it available for others? Yes, the notice by the holder will avail for every prior indorser of the bill who has a right of recourse against the party to whom the notice of dishonour has been given. Just meditate on this, and if you will refer to the list of indorsements which I gave you last week, look at the indorsement "William Robertson, pay Jonathan George." Jonathan George is assumed to be the holder of the bill. Suppose, therefore, "Jonathan George" to be the holder of the bill, and suppose him to give notice of dishonour to "William Hartly" and the other intermediate indorsers, then I tell you that every indorsee between the holder "Jonathan George" and "William Hartly," although such indorsee has not given any notice himself, can avail himself of the notice of dishonour that has been given to "William Hartly" to sue "William Hartly" and every indorser between himself and "Hartly." See the importance of that. It may be that "James Robinson," "George French" and "James Saunders" have neglected to give notice, but they find that the holder gave notice to "William Hartly." "Hartly" is a solvent man; that will do for them. Supposing they did not give notice to "Hartly" they can avail themselves of the notice that "Jonathan George" gave, and render thereby "Hartly" responsible. These things are in the case of the holder giving notice.

Then the next is as to an indorser giving notice. "Jonathan George" is the holder of the bill; he is the only person who could present it for payment by himself or his agent. He has presented it for payment; it has been dishonoured, brought back to his counting house. He has given notice of dishonour to "William Hartly," but forgotten to give notice of dishonour to "Thomas Daft." "William Hartly," on receipt of the notice, gives due notice of dishonour to "Thomas Daft." Such notice will enure for the benefit of the holder and all indorsers subsequent to "Thomas Daft." I do not know whether you follow me. Take first, the case in which the holder gives notice. Then such notice enures for his benefit, and all subsequent holders: and all indorsers, between the holder and the person to whom notice has been given, who have a right of recourse against such person, can avail themselves of the notice given by the holder. In the case of an indorser who gives notice, the notice he gives, if given within due time, will avail the holder and all indorsers subsequent to the party to whom notice is given.

Now let me pass on. What is notice of dishonour, and how may it be given? If you look at the notes to the case of *Bickerdike* v. *Bollman*, 2nd vol. Smith's Leading Cases, you will see some of the cases in which the question has been discussed. How can a notice of dishonour be given? Now it need not be given in writing. It need not be signed. It may be partly in writing and partly by word of mouth. You can do it all by word of mouth; or a defective communication by word of mouth in the morning supplemented by a further statement in the afternoon. Do please get these provisions in your minds. These are the things upon which, when I was called to the Bar, and when, in undefended actions on bills of exchange, every allegation material to the plaintiff's cause of action was traversed, men used to live. Actions on bills of exchange were far more numerous then than now. Actions upon them could be as speedily concluded then as they can be to-day, in spite of the supposed improvements in your procedure, and the expenses were less than your applications under Order 14, and the costly affidavits and allowances. As causes are now tried in some cases without pleadings, and every possible defence may be set up without much time for consideration, you must have your law, to use a common phrase, at your fingers' ends. You must be ready furnished to take a brief now, as we used in former days at Westminster Hall, at a moment's notice. In former days young counsel enjoyed a walk of twenty minutes away from chambers to find a solicitor waiting to deliver, at Westminster Hall, two or three small briefs marked undefended to be tried before a Judge who in defence of the absent defendant put counsel to the strictest proof of the various allegations traversed by the pleadings. Let it be present to your mind, that, for a notice of dishonour, all that is requisite is to intimate to the person who is to be charged that the bill has been presented for payment and has not been paid. It is not necessary that it should be in any particular form of words. You will not find it perhaps clearly and easily stated for you even in the Code. But take it as I have had it in my mind: Whatever the words—there is no set form of words requisite—it must intimate that the bill has been dishonoured by non-acceptance or non-payment. If the word dishonoured is used, such word will be quite sufficient, because the word dishonoured implies that it has been presented for acceptance or payment. It is not necessary to say expressly that the bill has been presented for payment or has been dishonoured. Any words that intimate the fact of dishonour will be sufficient. At one time it was thought that the notice of dishonour must also intimate that the person who gives the notice looks to the person to whom it is given for payment. It need do nothing of the kind. Read the case of *Solarte* v. *Palmer* (2 Clark and Finelly's Reports, p. 93), in which it was held that the following notice was not a notice of dishonour: "Gentlemen,— A bill for 683*l*., drawn by Joseph Keats upon Messrs. Daniel Jones & Co., and bearing your indorsement, has been put into our hands by the assignees of Mr. J. R. de Alzedo, with directions to take legal measures for the recovery thereof unless immediately paid to —— Gentlemen, your obedient servants, J. & S. Pearce." Of course the person who received the letter knew that the day for the meeting of the bill was past, but simply telling him that you will take legal proceedings against him does not tell him that it has really been presented for payment and is unpaid. A person may take or threaten legal proceedings against a man, although the bill has not been presented; yet somebody tried to argue that the holder could not take legal proceedings against a drawer or indorser unless the bill had been presented for payment and payment refused, and, therefore, the words contain by implication a notice that there has been a due presentment. The Court said "No," and I think, if I may say so, rightly, but the rule which was laid down in that case, viz. that a notice of dishonour ought in express terms or by necessary implication to convey full intimation that the bill has been dishonoured, seems to be too narrow. The statement of Baron Parke "That it is enough, if it appear by reasonable intendment and would be inferred by any man of business that the bill has been presented to the acceptor and not paid by him" has found a general acceptance with the modern judges. You may read in connection with *Solarte* v. *Palmer* the case of *Hartley* v. *Case*, 4 Barnewall and

Cresswell, p. 339. Many writers considered the decisions in these cases as being too technical, and in 1857 Mr. Justice Byles wrote, in the 7th edition of his work on Bills, "that the decisions in *Hartley* v. *Case* and *Solarte* v. *Palmer*, have been followed by no small inconvenience to the public, who are now hardly safe in giving notices of dishonour without professional aid." Mr. Justice Byles sets forth a number of cases in which the notice of dishonour was held insufficient, which seem to justify his opinion. But you may take it now that all technical rules relating to notice of dishonour are banished for ever. You need not let the drawer or indorser know that you look to him for payment,—you need not put your statement in any particular form; but you must let him know in some form or other that the bill has been dishonoured by non-payment. One of the cases which I generally look at, and which is a very good guide in the matter of giving notice of dishonour, is the case of *Paul* v. *Joel*. I have not troubled you with many cases, and perhaps if I should be able to publish my lectures, I shall not trouble you with any more. If you rely on a case, get a good one; but let it by careful study become yours, and a part of your intellectual being.

The case of *Paul* v. *Joel*, a decision of the Court of Exchequer Chamber, is reported in 3 Hurlstone and Norman, p. 455, and in 4 Hurlstone and Norman, p. 355. The bill had been duly presented for payment and been dishonoured. The notice of dishonour was written on a piece of paper and taken into the drawer. The notice ran thus: "B.'s acceptance to J., £500 due 12th January, is unpaid. Payment to R. & Co. is requested before 4 o'clock." That was held to be a sufficient notice of dishonour, because in saying that it was unpaid an ordinary person would understand that it was unpaid after presentation for payment in conformity with mercantile usage and legal obligation. Keep that case in your minds, and also the case of *Solarte* v. *Palmer*, in which case there was only a threat of legal proceedings, and they will guide you safely in determining when notice of dishonour has been duly given. The man of business in giving notice of dishonour should of course give the full and precise information of the bill, stating clearly its presentation and dishonour. The lawyer of course must be able to determine the least that may be given to constitute notice of dishonour. I may say that the communication will not be deemed a good notice of dishonour unless the terms sufficiently identify the bill. A mistake in describing the bill will not vitiate the notice unless the party to whom the notice is given has been misled thereby.

Now I must hasten on. Next I come to the time within which notice of dishonour must be given. The best way to state the rule as to time is thus, that as a general rule (as you may have to deal with foreign bills of exchange, and act in some cases of difficulty), notice of dishonour must be given within a reasonable time after the dishonour. Take that general proposition, because it may serve to guide you in other cases which do not come within the rules I am about to mention. By the law of England a reasonable time in certain cases has been fixed from which there can be allowed no departure, unless there are circumstances which excuse the giving notice altogether. By the law of England, if the bill has been dishonoured and the person you seek to charge lives in the same place as yourself, the notice must be given or sent off in time to reach him on the day after the dishonour of the bill. Therefore, if the holder is in London and a bill is dishonoured to-day, he must take care that notice reaches the drawer or indorser to-morrow if he lives in London. I do not think that it is necessary that the notice of dishonour should reach him in business hours, but it is best to take care that it reaches the drawer or indorser within business hours on the day following the dishonour. If the person whom you seek to charge does not reside in the same town, but in a different place, then you have the whole of the next day after the day of dishonour within which to post to him a proper communication of what has taken place. Keeping in mind the general rule that notice of dishonour must be given within a reasonable time after the dishonour, and the two rules I have just given you, you will not want more knowledge for the ordinary business to which you will be called. Permit me to say to you, do not be troubling your heads with difficult problems that may trouble the greatest judicial minds. Learn the ordinary and common, well-ascertained principles applicable to legal transactions. I have not spent much of my time in discussing doubtful problems. Get clearly in your minds the rules about which there is no dispute, and be ever ready to apply them. You must also be familiar with the excuses for not giving notice of dishonour in conformity with the rules I have just mentioned. Notice of dishonour is dispensed with when, after the exercise of reasonable care, notice cannot be given or cannot reach the drawer or indorser within the ordinary time. Notice of dishonour is excused by express or implied words of waiver. With respect to the drawer, notice is excused when drawee and drawer are the same person; also where the drawee is a fictitious person, or where the bill has been accepted for the accommodation of the drawer. If a bill is dishonoured in the hands of an agent either he or his principal may give notice of dishonour. If the agent gives notice of dishonour to his principal he must do it in the same time as if he were the holder giving notice to a drawer or indorser. The principal upon receipt of notice has the same time for giving notice as if the agent had been an independent holder. This, including what I have said in the former lectures, is all I can say to you about the general principles of law with regard to bills of exchange.

I must now offer a few observations on promissory notes and cheques. You will remember that very nearly all

I have been saying to you during the last two or three lectures in respect of bills of exchange is applicable to promissory notes. I desire, in addition, to make one or two observations on promissory notes which I trust may be useful to you. The ordinary form of a promissory note may be seen in the first of the two forms, No. 12, found on the pages preceding this Lecture. Now never forget this, that the maker of a promissory note as a rule stands in the position of, or answers to an acceptor of a bill of exchange; therefore unless the promise to pay in the body of the note is qualified by place, there is no occasion to present the note for payment in order to charge the maker, and of course notice of dishonour as to him has no place. The first indorser of a promissory note payable to a person other than the maker of the note stands in the position of the drawer of a bill, and such indorser has practically the same responsibilities and the same privileges as the indorser of a bill of exchange. To render such an indorser liable presentment for payment is necessary. An instrument in the form of a note payable to the maker's own order does not become a note until the maker indorses it. Such an instrument is seen in the second form printed on the page prior to this lecture. A promissory note may be made payable to bearer. A Bank of England note is a common instance of this. Having in your mind the provisions relating to Bills of Exchange, you can easily determine the various obligations imposed upon the persons who indorse promissory notes, and the various privileges which they enjoy. Then do not forget that a promissory note is incomplete until it is delivered to the payee or bearer. I have not made a promissory note when I have simply procured a stamped piece of paper, and written upon it, "I promise to pay A. B. £100 three months after date," and put my signature thereto. It is not a promissory note until I have delivered it with the intention of passing the property therein. The words I have just used constitute the common form of a promissory note, and the forms of bills of exchange and promissory notes are so well observed now that I can only recall one case in my practice in which an ambiguous instrument has been brought under my notice, calling for my opinion whether the instrument was a bill of exchange or a promissory note. Still you will study some of the cases to see when an instrument is a *bill of exchange*, and when it is a *promissory note*, by reason of certain irregularities in its inception.

Then a promissory note can be indorsed and dealt with exactly as if it were a bill of exchange—it can be indorsed in blank or specially indorsed, in the same manner as a bill of exchange. The obligations as to presentment for payment and notice of dishonour arise with respect to the first indorser if he is a person different from the maker of the promissory note, and to him notice must be given as to the drawer of a bill of exchange. If I promise to pay £100 to my own order (see second form, No. 13, preceding this Lecture), then, of course, it does not become a promissory note, and is not in existence truly as a promissory note until I put my indorsement upon it and deliver it, but in that case I shall not be a first indorser so as to entitle me to notice of dishonour. I am still the *maker* of the promissory note, and I am not entitled to notice of dishonour any more than the acceptor of a bill of exchange, to whom the maker of a promissory note answers. To charge an indorser of a promissory note presentment for payment is necessary, and also notice of dishonour. If a promissory note payable on demand has been indorsed, it must be presented for payment within a reasonable time of the indorsement, or the indorser will be discharged. If, however, a person takes a note for value which appears not to have been presented for payment within a reasonable time since its issue, the holder is only affected by defects of which he had notice, and is not affected by all the equities arising out of the note.

I now desire to say a few words to you about cheques.

A cheque relates as a rule to a banker, and comes into existence by his authority. It is drawn on the banker by a person who is styled his customer. The relation between a banker and his customer is only that of debtor and creditor. The banker has no money in his hands belonging to his customer where the customer pays in monies to his current account; and yet I have actually heard a very intelligent gentleman (since I began to lecture here) say that a banker to whom the customer has paid in monies on his current account, is a trustee of those monies. The banker has no monies of anybody except his own. Why, you know the contract of *mutuum* in the Roman law, at least you ought to know it. If I lend you money, the property becomes yours absolutely; and if a fire occurs and melts the five sovereigns I have lent you, you will still have to pay me five sovereigns, and the loss is yours. You may have *commodatum* even in respect of money; because if I lend you money, yet if I stipulate that the specific coins lent shall be returned to me, they do not become your property. The transaction is not *mutuum*; it is *commodatum*. But in the case of a banker, the transaction is *mutuum*; he is not to return you the actual sovereigns or notes handed over to him. If I have twelve Jubilee sovereigns, and I say, " I will lend them to you to exhibit in your window," they do not become yours. They are still mine, and I am the true owner of them, and you must return them when I ask for them. A banker as a rule has no money but what is his own. The customer lends him money, and the banker promises to re-pay him. How? He promises to discharge his obligation to his customer in a particular way. He says to his customer " Fill up, in a particular way, these pieces of paper, which constitute a cheque-book, and which I now hand to you: put your name as drawer to these pieces of paper, and until I have discharged my debt to you I will pay all the sums you write on those pieces of paper, to you or such person as you authorize to receive the money."

The relation between banker and customer is, as Lord Bramwell would often say, nothing but the relation of debtor and creditor, with the superadded obligation on the part of the banker to discharge the debt in a particular way. That is all. So much is this the case, that if you pay some money over the counter of a bank to the credit of your account which is not overdrawn, and a cashier at the bank has got his hand upon it, even if you should begin to suspect the solvency of the bank, you cannot take the money back. Equally remember this, that the moment the bank-clerk, when cashing a cheque, has placed notes or money within the control of the person presenting the cheque, the bank-clerk also cannot take back either money or notes; there is actual delivery and possession. The customer should always remember that if his account is very low and he should by chance draw a cheque for a larger amount than the bank owes, the bank may properly refuse to honour the cheque, and is not bound to offer to pay the sum actually due.

Now there is no acceptance of a cheque, nor does it require any, and no person can sue in respect of it the bank upon whom the cheque is drawn. It is given for immediate payment and is not entitled to days of grace. A cheque may be circulated, and, if necessary, indorsed, and the indorsee of a cheque may sue the drawer of the cheque just as the indorsee of a bill of exchange may sue the acceptor. Within my time, however, it was contended that an indorsee of a cheque could not sue the indorser thereon. In my time I have seen a lawyer who lived much in the past and studied in old books, a grand old black-letter lawyer, come down to the Court of Common Pleas to argue, in the year of grace 1860, that a cheque could not be indorsed so that the indorsee could maintain an action against the indorser. And if you wish to look at one of those long antiquarian arguments which when delivered excite the astonishment of people, look at the case of *Keene* v. *Beard*, which is reported in 8 C. B. N. S., p. 372. Mr. Grant contended in that case that a cheque was not to be classed with bills of exchange so far as to impose a liability on an indorser to the person who may be the holder. The Court held that a cheque was a negotiable instrument and capable of indorsement, and that the holder of a cheque could sue the indorser thereon. I shall never forget the quiet humour of Mr. Justice Byles, when, looking at Mr. Grant as a kind of Rip Van Winkle, he said: "I do no injustice to the able argument of Mr. Grant when I observe that it would have been deserving of more attention if it had been addressed to the Court a hundred years ago." Also remember that a cheque drawn by the customer does not, according to the law of England, constitute an assignment of any portion of the debt due from the banker. It is a simple request which the banker has promised to comply with; and if the banker (all things being in order) does not meet his engagement to pay, an action will lie by the customer against him for the non-performance of his obligation. The action may be either an action of tort or in contract, but the action is really founded upon the contract into which the banker has entered, and the customer, even if the action be in tort, founded upon the duty which the contract gives rise to, is entitled to nominal damages, although no actual loss has been sustained. Of course, the customer may recover considerable damages, although no proof is offered of any actual damage having followed the refusal to pay the cheque. Let me say to those of you who intend to practise in the Courts, if you want to get the law of torts in your minds, never place under the law of torts any obligation that arises out of contract. You will burthen your minds and memories too much if in trying to remember the various obligations that arise *ex delicto* you attempt to include amongst them any obligations arising *ex contractu*. Learn the great obligations which rest upon men, and which they have to perform apart from contract. They are to be found in decided cases or in statutes. They are many and sometimes difficult to ascertain. If, however, there is a contract, there must be an obligation, and to relieve my mind I put a great portion of the mass of obligations which rest upon railway companies, shipowners, and employments of all descriptions, as arising chiefly *ex contractu*. If you are asked whether an obligation exists in a particular case, let me tell you that the first thing you have to do when you look at your papers is to ask yourselves: " Is there any contract here ? " " I think there is," you may say. Then ascertain the terms of the contract and you will have little difficulty in ascertaining the nature and extent of the obligation. If you come to the conclusion that there is no obligation arising *ex contractu*, you must ask yourselves whether there is any obligation existing independently of contract. I cannot stay to discuss this matter fully tonight, but I say with respect to bankers the obligation to honour the customer's cheque rests upon a clear and distinct promise that they have made to him; it need not be expressed in actual words; it arises by implication from the course of business and the nature of the transaction. It is not necessary to prove any special damage for the purpose of maintaining an action for dishonouring a customer's cheque. You see this clearly if you keep to the question of contract. See what a help that is to you. In many cases of tort, unless there is sensible appreciable damage, there is no cause of action; but whether you get costs or not, of this you may be assured, that if you can allege a contract which the defendant has broken without excuse or justification the plaintiff is entitled to some damages. Then remember this, that in the case of a man in a large way of business he may be entitled to substantial damages for the refusal to pay his cheque. Therefore, bankers' clerks should be very careful to see that everything that a customer has paid in has been put to his credit, in order that the paying cashier may commit no mistake or blunder; but when you have committed one, make peace with your customer as soon as you possibly can. If he is a decent man he will not bring an action against his banker unless he has received some serious injury. Injury arising from the dishonour of a cheque is to a large extent imaginary; and yet in one case in our books, without proof of any special damage, a jury gave £500 damages against a bank for dishonouring a cheque, but the Court reduced the damages to £200. In the last case I was in for dishonouring a cheque, the jury said they found that the plaintiff had sustained no damage. "But you must give nominal damages for the breach of contract," said the judge. And the jury assessed the damages at 1s. I should tell you that the defendants having paid £25 into Court, judgment was entered for the defendants, and an order was made for the repayment of £24 19s. 0d. to the bank, and an order that the plaintiff do pay the bankers all the costs of the action.

Do not forget that whilst cheques can be drawn and indorsed, the person who holds the cheque cannot bring any action against the banker in case he refuse to pay it. It is the customer, the person who is entitled to draw the cheque and use it, who alone can maintain any action against the banker for dishonouring the cheque. The banker has not accepted: he can laugh at the holder and say, "Take this piece of paper away; I have nothing to do with *you*. My customer, to whom I gave the cheque book, and who is authorised to use it, can complain, and he alone." I may say to you that there can be a *special indorsement* as well as an indorsement in blank of a cheque just as of a bill of exchange.

Cheques can be drawn to "bearer" or to "order." I should tell you that the post-dating of a cheque drawn to order does not affect its validity in the slightest. It is a perfectly valid instrument, and a person who takes it *bonâ fide* and for value has a perfectly good title.

This was decided by Mr. Justice Wills and the Court of Appeal in the case of the *Royal Bank of Scotland* against *Tottenham*, 1894, 2 Queen's Bench, 715, which really followed the decision of *Whistler* v. *Forster*, in 14 C. B. N. S., p. 248. Mr. Justice Wills decided that the definition of a cheque given in the Bills of Exchange Act, 1882, had in no way affected the previous decisions as to post-dated cheques.

A cheque payable to "order" gave rise in former days to important questions between customer and banker. The customer might say to the banker: "I find you have debited my account with the payment of one hundred pounds on a particular day. Why have you done so?" The banker replies, because he had honoured a cheque of the customer for that amount. The customer may answer: "Let me look at my cheque." It is produced, and the customer at once says: "That payment was not made at my request. The cheque is drawn in favour of Richard Johnson. The signature on the back of the cheque is not his. It is a forgery. You have not followed my mandate. You must strike out from my account that payment of one hundred pounds." "I paid it honestly," says the banker. "I dare say you did, but you have not followed my authority." Prior to the 16th & 17th Victoria, cap. 59, sec. 19, the banker was obliged to strike the one hundred pounds from the pass-book as a payment and bear the loss, if any, occasioned by the forgery himself. By section 19 of that Act it is provided that any draft or order drawn upon a banker for a sum of money payable to order on demand which shall, when presented for payment, purport to be indorsed by the person to whom the same shall be drawn payable, shall be a sufficient authority to such banker to pay the amount of such draft or order to the bearer thereof; and it shall not be incumbent on such banker to prove that such indorsement or any subsequent indorsement was made by the direction or authority of the payee or by the drawer or any indorser of the draft drawn to order. Thus the law was altered, and now every banker who pays a cheque honestly and fairly is entitled to charge the sum he pays to the account of the customer even although the signature of the payee or an indorser be forged—a very great and substantial protection to the banker. Do not suppose for a moment that the banker can charge to the account of his customer the amount of a cheque bearing the forged signature of the customer, and which the banker has paid. This he cannot do. He must know his customer's signature. The Act of 16 & 17 Vict. c. 59 only protects the banker upon whom the cheque is drawn in case *he* pays a cheque on which an indorsement has been forged. Any banker or individual who has obtained the money for which the cheque is drawn, by presenting the cheque with a forged indorsement to the banker on whom the cheque is drawn, must return the money so obtained to the customer. See the case of *Ogden* v. *Benas*, L. R. 9 C. P., p. 513. If the amount of the cheque has been altered and made payable for a larger sum since the customer drew it, the banker cannot place the forged amount to the debit of the customer, but only the sum for which the cheque was originally drawn. If any negligent conduct of the drawer has directly led to the alteration of the bill, the customer must bear the loss himself, if there has been no want of care on the part of the banker in cashing the cheque.

In connexion with this I will mention one case which, I think, has been much misunderstood. The case is *Young* v. *Grote*, 4 Bingham 253, a case which in my opinion was properly decided. The case deals with the relation of banker and customer, and involves the question whether, where a cheque has been altered to represent a larger sum than that for which it was originally drawn, opportunity for such alteration being afforded by the careless way in which the cheque was drawn, the banker can charge his customer's account with the full amount which he paid under what seemed the customer's cheque. If he himself has not been guilty of any negligence in paying, I think he can, by virtue of the contract into which the customer enters. If the banker promises the customer that he will pay upon the presentation of his cheque, I think the customer promises the banker that he will take reasonable care, in filling up the instrument, to see that it is filled up in such a way that opportunity for alteration of the cheque by the insertion of other words and figures shall not exist. I have always thought that obligation was well established. Moreover, there is a principle of law which says that no man shall ever be allowed to impute to another that loss which is due to his own want of reasonable care, even although there be no legal duty to exercise reasonable care incumbent upon him, for breach of which an action would lie. This principle is recognised as well in actions of contract as in actions of tort, is not confined to cases of negligence, but extends also to claims arising out of contract. Although a man is under no obligation to take reasonable care, and no one could sue him for not doing so, yet, if ever he comes into Court to demand something from an opponent, or to put upon another a loss he himself has sustained, he shall not impute to that opponent the damage or the loss which is due to his own want of reasonable care. In my opinion, *Young* v. *Grote* may be sustained on both these grounds.

Now in the case of *Young* v. *Grote*, what were the facts? Peter Young, the plaintiff, kept an account with the defendants, Grote & Company, the well-known bankers. They had given him a cheque-book, and were in the habit of honouring the cheques he drew upon them. On the 12th August, 1826, Young was leaving home, and as there were payments to be made in his absence on account of his business, he signed with his name five of the printed cheques without inserting in them any dates or sums of money. He gave these cheques to his wife, telling her to fill them up for such sums as the business might require. On the 19th August it was necessary to use one of the cheques, and the wife requested a clerk of Young's to fill up one of the cheques with the sum of fifty pounds two shillings and three pence. The clerk filled up the cheque for that amount, but in such a way as to allow of the cheque being easily made to appear to be drawn for a larger amount. The cheque as drawn was shown to Mrs. Young, who sanctioned its being issued in the way the clerk had drawn it. The clerk was told by Mrs. Young to get the cheque cashed. Before taking it to the bankers, the clerk altered the cheque, so as to make it appear to be a cheque drawn for three hundred and fifty pounds. It was presented to the cashier at the bank as a cheque drawn for three hundred and fifty pounds, and was paid as such. It was found as a fact that the bankers' clerk had not been guilty of any negligence in cashing the cheque, as a cheque drawn for three hundred and fifty pounds. The bankers debited Young's account with the sum of three hundred and fifty pounds. Young objected to this amount, and said he ought only to be charged with the sum of fifty pounds ten shillings and threepence. The question in the case was, who should lose the three hundred pounds, the customer or the bankers? It was found as a fact that the careless way in which the cheque had been drawn afforded the opportunity for making the alteration. The Court decided that the loss must, under the circumstances, fall upon the customer, Young. It is not easy to ascertain, from the language of the judges, the precise grounds on which the Court proceeded in giving judgment for the bankers. Some have said that the decision rests upon the doctrine of estoppel. Such a word as estoppel is not found in the judgments, and it seems to me impossible to rest the judgment upon any such ground. Some have said that the judgment rests upon the principle that a man who puts his name to a blank cheque is responsible for the amount which may be inserted by the person to whom it is delivered. It is difficult to accept this as the ground of the decision, because, although the plaintiff put his signature to a blank cheque, it was not issued as a blank cheque. It was filled up and drawn for fifty pounds before his agent, his wife, parted with the possession of the cheque. I think the decision can only rest upon the grounds I have already indicated. If once it is admitted that there was a duty to exercise reasonable care in filling up the cheque, I think the loss was, in *Young* v. *Grote*, the direct consequence of the breach of duty. If, however, any intelligent cashier, looking at the cheque, would have his suspicions aroused and decline to cash the cheque, then the negligence of the customer has not caused the loss. It is a question what damage the customer's want of reasonable care has occasioned, and if, exercising reasonable care, an ordinarily prudent banker would not have paid on the cheque, the customer's negligence has not occasioned the damage; it is the want of care of the banker that has caused the loss.

Now there is another case, closely allied to *Young* v. *Grote*, I should just like to mention to you. It is the case of *Scholfield* v. *Earl of Londesborough*, reported in the Court of Appeal, in Law Reports, 1895, 1 Queen's Bench, p. 536. In that case Lord Londesborough accepted a bill drawn for five hundred pounds in such a way that the drawer could easily turn it into a bill for a larger amount. The drawer did, after the acceptance, turn it into a bill for three thousand five hundred pounds. The drawer parted with the bill, and it ultimately came into the hands of the plaintiff as a bill honestly and truly accepted for three thousand five hundred pounds. It was admitted or proved that the plaintiff took the bill *bonâ fide* or for value. The plaintiff sought to make the defendant liable as an acceptor of a bill for three thousand five hundred pounds. The defendant admitted his liability for five

hundred pounds, and brought that sum into Court.
There was a division of opinion among the judges in
the Court of Appeal as to the defendant's liability.
The Master of the Rolls and Lord Justice Rigby were
of opinion that there was not any legal duty on the
defendant to take reasonable care to see that the bill
before he accepted it was in such a state as not to
admit of its alteration by the insertion of other words
and figures. They also intimated their opinion that if
there was such a duty, there was no evidence of any
negligence on the part of the defendant, and that the
loss was not the direct result of the breach of duty, if
such duty existed. Lord Justice Lopes held that there
was such a duty, that there was evidence of its breach,
and that the loss was the direct result of the breach of
duty. This case is distinguishable from *Young* v. *Grote*
on two grounds, viz., that there was no contractual
relation of any kind between the plaintiff and Lord
Londesborough, and that Lord Londesborough was
not seeking to put any liability or loss on the plaintiff
which otherwise he, Lord Londesborough, would have
to bear. If I may be permitted to say so, I think
there was no such duty cast upon Lord Londesborough
as that laid down by Lord Justice Lopes, but if there
be such a duty, then I think that the loss was the
direct result of such breach of duty. No doubt, ordinarily, the damage which arises from the voluntary act
of a person cannot be imputed as damage resulting
from the breach of duty resting upon another and
different person; but I do not think this rule applies
where the duty exists for the purpose of preventing
loss by the act or acts of other persons. The case is
under appeal to the House of Lords, and the questions
arising on it, questions of the utmost importance, will
be finally determined. I hope their decision will leave
Young v. *Grote* a binding authority, affording protection
to bankers, who are entitled to ask, as it seems to me,
that their customers shall take reasonable care to fill
up the cheques so that their use shall not involve

the bankers in any loss, against which by reasonable diligence on their part they could not protect themselves.

Now I have just a word or two to say with respect to crossed cheques, and then I have done. With respect to crossed cheques, you can go to the Act of 1882 and see all the provisions there collected. I should like you, however, instead of reading at once in the Code the sections relating to crossed cheques, to do this: just to take in their proper order the Acts of Parliament themselves by which the alterations in the law were successively effected. The provisions in the Code without illustration will seem uninviting and appear to present in the bulk greater difficulties than the matter really involves. The first Act which relates to the crossing of bank cheques is the 19th & 20th Victoria, cap. 25, sec. 1. Then came the 21st & 22nd Victoria, cap. 79, sec. 1; and then the Crossed Cheques Act of 1876, 39 & 40 Vict. c. 81. By reading these Acts you will see how the law as to the crossing of cheques or drafts on bankers has grown. The Act of 1856, 19 & 20 Vict. c. 25, stated in the preamble that doubts had arisen as to the obligations of bankers with respect to cross-written drafts, and that it would conduce to the ease of commerce if drawers or holders of drafts on bankers payable to bearer or to order on demand were enabled to direct the payment of the same to be made only to or through some banker. It then enacts that in every case where such a draft bears across its face an addition of the name of any banker or of the words "and Company," in full or abbreviated, either of such directions shall have the force of a direction to the bankers that the draft is to be paid only to or through some banker, and shall be payable only to or through some banker. The result of this Act was, that if the cheque presented to the banker was crossed with the name of any banker or the words "& Co.," and he paid the cheque to any person other than *a* banker, he could not charge his customer's account with such payment. The customer could waive the provision of this Act if he chose, and allow the sum paid to be charged to his account, although the payment was contrary to the banker's duty. By the Act of 1858, 21 & 22 Vict. c. 79, the crossing of a cheque or draft became a material part of the cheque or draft, and if a cheque was issued crossed with a banker's name it imposed the obligation on the banker on whom the cheque or draft was drawn of paying the cheque only to *the* banker with whose name the cheque was crossed. The statute also enables the holder of a cheque issued uncrossed, or crossed only with the words "& Co.," to cross the same with the name of a banker; the holder of a cheque may by this act, where it has been issued uncrossed, cross the same with the words " and Co." In such cases the obligation of the banker is the same as if the cheque had been issued crossed in the way the holder has crossed it. There is also a provision that if the cheque when presented for payment does not plainly appear to have been crossed or to have been obliterated or altered, the customer shall not question any payment made by the banker on such a cheque, provided the banker has acted in good faith and without negligence. The chief advance by this Act is, that if a cheque is crossed with a banker's name, the payment must be made to such banker and no one else, and that a lawful holder of a cheque may cross a cheque in the same way as the person drawing it may cross it, and if no banker's name is on the cheque he may cross it with the name of a banker. By the Crossed Cheques Act, 1876, both the foregoing Acts were repealed, but their provisions, with some important additions, were re-enacted. By the Act of 1876 two parallel transverse lines simply constitute a crossing. A name is given to the crossing where a banker's name forms part of the crossing. Such cheque is to be deemed a cheque "specially crossed." It also authorises a banker to whom a cheque is specially crossed, to cross it specially to another banker, his agent, for collection. This Act prohibits payment of a cheque crossed specially more than once, except where the second crossing is to a banker for the purpose of making him an agent for collection on behalf of the banker whose name has been written across the cheque. But do not forget this—there is nothing to prevent a customer from waiving the mistake of the banker in paying a crossed cheque, and if the money has been obtained from the banker under such circumstances that the banker could recover back the money, the customer can recover it. In this connexion I would ask you to look at the case of *Bobbett* v. *Pinkett*. It is reported in L. R. 1 Ex. D., p. 373. Bobbett was a customer of the Lewes Old Bank, Molineux & Co. Bobbett, on 14 December, 1874, gave a cheque for £47 16s. 11d. to a man named Pennack, residing at Birmingham, payable to his order, in payment for some goods that had been supplied to Bobbett, the cheque being crossed "London and County Bank." Pennack left the cheque with other papers on the desk of a commercial room. He turned to his friends for the conversation of the evening, and a gentleman, who was sitting by, who was a little hard up, just put his hand among the papers, and seeing there was a cheque amongst them, stole it. This gentleman passed from Birmingham to Worcester, and went to Mr. Pinkett's hotel. He stayed there for some days. Then he forged the signature of Pennack, to whom the cheque was payable, and asked the landlord at the house where he was staying to cash it. Pinkett before doing so telegraphed to Molineux to know whether the cheque was all right and would be paid. Molineux replied that the cheque was good and would be paid unless they had orders not to pay it. Upon this, Pinkett cashed the cheque and gave the money to the guest. He paid his hotel-bill out of the money, and went his way with the rest. Pennack communicated his loss to the plaintiff on or about the 15th of December, and on the 29th the

plaintiff sent Pennack another cheque for the same
amount. Pinkett paid the cheque into his account
with the Worcester City Banking Co. They forwarded
it to the London Joint Stock Bank, who crossed
the cheque payable to themselves. Molineux paid
the cheque to the London Joint Stock Bank, not
observing or disregarding the name of the London and
County Bank, with which the cheque had been crossed
by the drawer. The amount was charged to the account
of Bobbett by Molineux. The question was, "Could
the money which Pinkett had received be recovered?"
An opinion was given that it could, and that Mr.
Bobbett should recognise the payment that Molineux
had made, and waive the benefit of the provisions of the
Acts relating to crossed cheques. He did so, and the
payment made by Molineux became his payment when
he approved it. It was done on his behalf you cannot
doubt, when the cheque was paid by Molineux & Co.,
and therefore when he said, " I approve it," his account
could be charged, and his account was charged. Upon
this it seemed clear that Mr. Pinkett, of Gloucester, by
his agents the bankers, had obtained Mr. Bobbett's
money by presenting a cheque with a forged indorsement to Mr. Bobbett's agents, and that Mr. Bobbett
could bring an action against Pinkett to recover the
money paid by Molineux. The action was brought,
and without troubling you with all the facts, the jury, at
the trial before Baron Bramwell, found Pennack guilty
of negligence in losing the cheque and in not taking
steps to stop the cheque earlier than he did. They
found the plaintiff guilty of negligence in not
stopping the first cheque as soon as he knew of the
loss, and Molineux & Co. guilty of negligence in disregarding the name of the London and County Bank,
which was in their own customer's handwriting. The
jury acquitted the defendant of all negligence in giving
value for the cheque in the way he did. Counsel for
the defendant submitted that the action would not lie
because the plaintiff could not approbate the payment

by Molineux & Co. and complain of the payment to the defendant through his agent the London Joint Stock Bank. This argument and the findings of the jury as to negligence induced the learned judge to enter a verdict for the defendant. A rule *nisi* pursuant to leave reserved was obtained to set aside the verdict for the defendant and to enter it for the plaintiff, and the rule, after long argument and time taken for consideration, was made absolute. The plaintiff recovered the full amount of the cheque which had been charged to his account. Mr. Baron Bramwell very shortly disposed of the arguments as to approbating and reprobating the same matter by saying, " The plaintiff does not approbate and reprobate the same matter—the plaintiff approbates the mode of presentment but reprobates the defendant's title."

By the provisions of the Act of 1876, a drawer or a lawful holder may add to the crossing the words "not negotiable," and a person taking a crossed cheque with the words "not negotiable" on the face of it, acquires no better title than the person had from whom he took it. This, my last observation to you, brings me to the word with the true meaning of which I commenced my lectures. I early impressed upon you the importance of negotiability in respect of bills of exchange, promissory notes and cheques, and now I have to say that from cheques the attribute of negotiability can be withdrawn by a compliance with the provisions of the Act of 1876, which have been reproduced in the Codifying Act of 1882. Thus I end, as I started, with the question of negotiability. And that last word is a fit conclusion to the lectures I have delivered to you, which commenced with the endeavour to ascertain the true meaning of the word " negotiable."

Before we separate, permit me to say that I am much obliged to you for your constant presence and attention. I have been honoured by being permitted to speak to you. To those of you who are, or intend to become, members of my own profession, I should like to say that if I have rendered you any service by the exposition of the general principles of the law relating to negotiable instruments, or if, as the result of my lectures, you will leave this room determined to prosecute your studies with greater devotion, I shall be more than repaid. If any of you are not men of genius, and I hope you are not, but are industrious, plodding men, then the condition of our law, spread over many hundred volumes, should give you the greatest encouragement. Industry will master its chief decisions, reading them again and again with self-distrust; while genius will neglect them or in haste misapprehend them. Work, work while it is yet day, and in your lives let there be no misspent hours. Had I known when I was a student that I should live to receive the distinguished honour of speaking to you upon law, and stimulating you to the true and just exercise of your profession, I would have laboured more earnestly to present myself before you as a truly qualified teacher.

INDEX.

ACCEPTANCE,
  forms of, 107, 109
    See BILL OF EXCHANGE, ACCEPTANCE.
  may be conditional, 108, 113

ACCEPTOR. *See* BILL OF EXCHANGE.
  two or more persons may be jointly, but not successively, or alternatively, 106
  no one can be unless bill addressed to him, 116
  except where address but no name inserted in left hand corner and person living at address signs as acceptor, 118

ACCOMMODATION. *See* BILL OF EXCHANGE.
  acceptance, notice of dishonour of not necessary to charge drawer, 116, 157
    why not necessary, 158
    when not necessary to charge indorser, 159
  paper, warning against creating, 61

ACCOUNT STATED, not sufficient consideration for promise to pay in futuro, 70

ASSIGNMENT OF DEBT.
  See BILL OF EXCHANGE, assignment of debt by, 72 *et seq.*
  See CHOSE IN ACTION, 74 *et seq.*

BACON, V.-C., decision of in Percival *v.* Dunn, 72

BANKER,
  difference between instrument taken for collection by, and instrument taken for debt due to, 127
  relation to customer that of debtor to creditor, 169
  with superadded obligation to discharge debt in a particular way, 170
  not a trustee of money paid in by customer to current account, 169
  transaction with, resembles *mutuum*, not commodatum, of Roman law, 169
  there may be commodatum even in respect of money, 170
  how debt to customer ordinarily discharged, 170
  cannot take back money delivered to customer, 170
  customer cannot take back money delivered to, 170
  duty of to honour cheque arises from promise express or implied, 173
  customer only can sue, for refusal to honour cheque, 174
  action against either in contract or tort, but founded on contract, 172

BANKER—*continued.*
   formerly not entitled to debit customer with amount of cheque if indorsement forged, 175
   now otherwise (16 & 17 Vict. c. 59, sect. 19), 175
   not entitled to charge customer, if signature to cheque forgery, 175

BENJAMIN, Mr.
   skilful argument of, in Goodwin *v.* Robarts, 45

BILL OF EXCHANGE,
   importance of obtaining, in business transaction, 59
   readily convertible in money market of London, 59
   necessity for entering, in bills payable book, 60
   and for keeping in proper order, 60
   accommodation, warning against creating, 61
   necessity for care in dealing with, 61
   cannot exist, without drawer's name, inserted by person expressly or impliedly authorised, 63
   instrument appearing to be a, and to be in order, every signature genuine and honestly placed, will not give bona-fide holder for value remedy against supposed acceptor, unless drawer's name inserted by the acceptor's authority, 63
   marginal figures, not an essential part of a, 63
   words denoting the amount, are an essential part of a, 64
   alteration of figures in a, not a material alteration, so as to avoid instrument, 64
   acceptor of must be drawee, 64
   law as to, codified by Bills of Exchange Act, 1882, 45 & 46 Vict. c. 61, 65
   definition of, in Act, 65
   transactions which cannot be carried out by a, but which are valid at common law, 66 *et seq.*
   transactions which can be carried out by a, but which cannot be carried out by common law, or equity, 66 *et seq.*
   under what head of contract it comes, 66
   is a simple contract, 67
   instrument under seal not a, 67
   illustrates elements of agreement under simple contract, request, consideration, promise, with intention of entering into binding engagement, 67
   consideration for, if it exists, it does not matter from whom it moves, 67
   differs in that respect from other simple contracts, 68
   consideration for, is always presumed, 68
         may be shown not to have existed, 69
         what may be, 125
   must relate to debt, and debt only, in strictest sense of word, 69
   must be for fixed sum, 69, 102, 113
   request must not be conditional, 69
   conditional instrument not less invalid as, even if event should happen before expiration of the time mentioned in instrument, for performance of obligation, 70
   fixes time for payment beyond all dispute, 70
   constitutes conditional payment, 70
   days of grace for payment, 71
   unless payable on demand, 71
   definition of, not asked for in courts of law, 71
   gives rise to a claim for interest from maturity usually at 5%, 71

BILL OF EXCHANGE—*continued.*
    enables transactions which could be carried out at common law to be carried out with greater powers and facilities, 72
    assignment of debt by, 72, 73
    holder of may sue acceptor whereas holder of authority to pay cannot sue debtor, 72
    what generally appears on face of, 73
    back of, ordinarily relates to assignment of debt, 73
        contains names and signatures by which the debt is assigned, 73
    value of, and utility of, for mercantile transactions, increased by names added, 73
    differs herein from instruments at common law and equity, 73
    assignee of debt by indorsement of a, has advantages over assignee at common law, 75
    need not give to any parties to the bill notice of indorsement to him, 75
    indorsee of, before maturity, if holder for value, does not take subject to equities affecting previous holders, 76
    indorsee of, for value, is entitled to the amount upon the bill as against all precedent parties even if there has been fraud or deceit in the inception or transfer of the bill, or no real transaction to which the bill relates, 77
    most important incident of, the securing assignment of debt in a safe and simple manner, 97
    transferee of, safe from doubts as to equities attaching to debt, 97
    person taking, honestly and for value, unaffected by anything which took place between previous parties to instrument, 99
    if no consideration for, no action between immediate parties to, 99
    form of, explained, 100
    drawer of, who, 100
    drawee, person to whom bill addressed, 100
    instrument containing names of drawer and drawee, a perfect, although no acceptance, 100
    use of, in early times to discharge obligations in distant places, 101
        illustration, 101
    cannot exist, without drawee, 101, 108
    inland, 101
    not invalid, because drawer and drawee reside in same town, 102
    not necessary to validity of, that place of business or residence of drawer, or acceptor, or any place be inserted, 102
        or place of payment stated, 102
    date not necessary in, 102
        may be filled in, by bonâ-fide holder, 102
    no objection can be taken that date has been improperly filled in, if filled in before bill comes to bonâ-fide holder, 102
    figures in, controlled by words, 102
    amount of, must be fixed, but may be payable by instalments, 102
    according to Pothier must have three parties, drawer, drawee, payee, 104
    three parties not required by English law, 104
    nor by French law at present time, 104
    drawer may be payee, 104
        this illustrates the wisdom with which the Judges have built up the law, following all the needs of commerce, 104
    may be drawn " pay to bearer," 105

BILL OF EXCHANGE—*continued*
  meaning of "after date," 105
            "after sight," 105
            "at sight," 105
            "on demand," 105
            "on presentation," 105
  inland, defined, 105
  foreign, what is, 106
  two or more persons, not partners, may be drawers, drawees or acceptors of, 106
    jointly, but not successively or alternatively; they constitute as it were one drawer or drawee of bill, 106
  non-acceptance of, by drawee, who can sue for, 106
  who can be sued on non-accepted, 106
  acceptance of, ordinary form, 107
  acceptance of, must be in writing, as to English bills, since 1 & 2 Geo. 4, c. 78, 107
        foreign bills since 19 & 20 Vict. c. 97, 107
        may be qualified, 108, 114
    four forms of, 109
  instrument without a drawer not a, 101, 108
    such instrument should not be called acceptance in blank, or inchoate bill, 109
    practical importance of calling such an instrument by right name, 110
  drawing of, does not relate back to acceptance, 111
  person taking instrument on which no drawer's name appears, runs risk that person from whom he took had no authority to insert a drawer's name, 112
  drawing of, never conditional or qualified, 113
  acceptance of, may be conditional or qualified, 113
    but must not involve obligation to do other than pay fixed sum of money, 113
    by French law cannot be conditional, 113
  must not be contingent as to time, 114
  but may be payable a certain time after a contingent event which must happen, 114
  qualified acceptance of, person takes at his own risk, and must give notice to prior parties, 115
        if prior parties do not dissent, they continue liable, 115
        may be refused, and holder may treat bill as dishonoured by non-acceptance, 115
  drawn in favour of payee, change made by Act of 1882 in law relating to, 115
  acceptor of, no one can be, unless bill addressed to him, 116
    except where an address but no name is put in left hand corner of bill, and person living at the address signs the bill as acceptor, 118
  drawn by a man upon himself, perfectly good, 118
    but is, at the election of the holder, either a bill of exchange or a promissory note, 118
  acceptance may be on the back of a, 125
  indorsement may be on the face of a, 125
  given either on account of a pre-existing debt or in pursuance of a promise made when debt arose is given for value or for consideration, 126

BILL OF EXCHANGE—*continued*.
    title of creditor to, given for pre-existing debt formerly supposed to rest on implied agreement on his part to suspend his remedies, 126
    conditional payment of debt, 127
    operates as absolute payment until condition defeated, 127
    payable on demand, existing debt decided by four judges in *Currie* v. *Misa*, to be a sufficient consideration for, 128
        enacted in Bills of Exchange Act, 1882, s. 27, sub-s. b, 129
    drawn without consideration no action on by drawer against acceptor, 129
    or if transferred without value, by transferee against acceptor, 129
    in action on, absence of consideration between acceptor and drawer, and between holder and drawer must be alleged and proved, 129
        burden of proving these allegations rests on defendant who alleges them, 129
    negotiated, objection to terms as used in Bills of Exchange Act, 1882, 130
    transfer of, how it may be effected, 130
    delivery of, what not sufficient to pass property, 130
        must be with intention of passing property, 130
    law relating to, involves principles of almost every department of law, 131
        involves law of principal and agent, 131
    delivery of, part of the law of conveyance, 131
        to agent, is equivalent to delivery to principal, 131
    indorsee of, though not originally a party, may by the Law Merchant sue the acceptor upon contract entered into by him with the drawer, 131
    no person can be sued on, who does not put his name to, 133
    warranties by person transferring, for value, without putting his name to, and obligations outside, 134
    indorsement of, 134
        blank, 134, 138
        special, 134, 138
    indorsed in blank, transferable by mere delivery, 135
    indorsed specially, not transferable by delivery, or without indorsement, 135
    indorsed in blank, name of transferor not essential, to pass property in, 135
        essential if desired to make him party to bill, 135
    indorsers of, names of intervening may be struck out, 136
    person may be party to, in several capacities, 136
    acceptor of, if indorsee, cannot charge any antecedent party who would have remedy against him as acceptor, 136
    name of indorsee of, may be written by a person who does not make himself liable on, 137
    conditional indorsement of, may be disregarded under Act of 1882, 138
    indorsement of, cannot be partial, 139
        may be restrictive, 139
        examples of, 139
    overdue, 139
    disgraced, 140
        person takes subject to all equities arising out of original transaction, 140
        what are such equities, 140, 141

BILL OF EXCHANGE—*continued.*
  presentment of,
    must take place within a reasonable time, 146
    for acceptance, 146
    when must be made, 146
    by whom made, 147
    must be made to drawee at a reasonable hour on a business day and before bill is overdue, 147
    when excused, 146, 147
    for payment must be duly made, 153
    or reasonable diligence exercised to find acceptor or his agent in order to present, 153
    how effected, 153
    must be made on day bill falls due, 154
    difficulty of deciding when to be made, when bill payable on demand, 154
    to charge drawer, must be made within reasonable time after issue, 154
    to charge indorser, must be made a reasonable time after indorsement, 154
    should be made at once, 155
    if bill payable at sight and not accepted, must be made in order to get date from which bill is to run, 155
    after, and notice of non-acceptance, cause of action arises against drawer and indorsers, 155
    must be by holder, or some person authorised to receive payment on his behalf, 155
    must be made on a business day and at a reasonable hour, 155
    not necessary to charge acceptor, 155
      unless acceptance qualified, as to place, 155
    necessary to charge drawer and indorsers, 156
    where it must be made, 156
    to two or more persons, not partners, 157
    when excused, 157
    not excused by belief that bill will be dishonoured, 157
    not necessary where drawee fictitious, 157
        or to charge drawer where drawn for accommodation of drawer, 157
        why not necessary in this case, 158
    if not made, drawer and indorsers discharged, 159
    except in case of accommodation, 159
  dishonour of,
    notice of, must be given, 159
      by whom it must be given, 159
      any holder may avail himself of, 159
    does not prevent transfer, 160
    transferee after, takes subject to equities, 160
  dishonoured, what word implies, 163
  notice of dishonour of,
    who can avail himself of, 160
    what is, 161
    need not be in writing, 161
    or signed, 161
    may be partly written, partly oral, 161
    need merely intimate that bill has been presented for acceptance or payment, and has not been accepted or paid, 162
    any words sufficient which intimate fact of dishonour, 163
    technicalities as to, banished, 164

BILL OF EXCHANGE—*continued.*
   notice of dishonour of—*continued.*
      not good, unless its terms sufficiently define bill, 165
      must be given within reasonable time, 165
      cases in which reasonable time has been fixed, 165
      excused when after exercise of reasonable care it cannot be given, 166
         by waiver express or implied, 166
         when drawer and drawee same person, 166
            drawee fictitious, 166
            accepted for accommodation of drawer, 166
      agent in whose hands bill is must give, to his principal in same time as if he were holder giving notice to drawer or indorser, 166
      principal has then same time to give, as if agent were independent holder, 166

BILL OF LADING,
   not a negotiable instrument, 56
   difference between a, and a bill of exchange, 56
   transfer of a, will pass the entire property or a portion of the property according to the intention of the parties, 56
   prior to 18 & 19 Vict. c. 111 no one could sue on contract contained in a, unless originally a party to contract, 57

BLACKBURN, LORD,
   definition by, of *bona fides* in *Jones* v. *Gordon*, 26
   judgment of (when Blackburn, J.) in *Crouch* v. *Crédit Foncier*, analyzed, 35
   held that a debenture of an English public company is not a negotiable instrument, 36
   some of the earliest reporting work of, in Queen's Bench Reports, 39

BONA FIDES,
   constructive notice does not enter into consideration of meaning of, in speaking of *bonâ-fide* holder, 17
   carelessness not inconsistent with, 22
      must be considered in determining existence of, 22
   consideration given, a criterion of, 22, 144
   question of, where consideration is past may involve great care, 26
   suggestions as to dealing with question of, 25, 145

BONA-FIDE HOLDER,
   whether man is, depends on what knowledge he had, not on what he might or ought to have had, or what inquiries he ought to have made, 16
      this view recognised by House of Lords in *Simmons* v. *London Joint Stock Bank*, 16
      depends on what he did suspect, not on what he ought to have suspected, 16, 31
      depends on what was the state of his mind, not what would have been the state of another man's mind, in same circumstances, 16
   person having, at the time he takes a negotiable instrument, a suspicion that there is something wrong on the part of the person with whom he is dealing, not a, 25
   not necessary to show that he knew the exact wrong committed, 25
   may have obtained instrument from person whom he knew to be an agent, if he believed him to have authority to deal with it, 29

BOWEN, LORD,
    use by, of phrase "negotiability by estoppel," 14
    opinion of, that share-warrants in English companies are not negotiable, 49
    decided in *Garrard* v. *Lewis* that words denoting amount so far controlled figures in a bill, that figures are not a material part of the instrument, 103

BRAMWELL, LORD,
    expressions used by, in *Sheffield* v. *London Joint Stock Bank*, seem to give ground for opinion that *bonâ-fide* holder of a negotiable instrument may be affected with constructive notice, 15
    grounds of judgment of, in *Goodwin* v. *Robarts*, 46

BROOM, MR.,
    ignorance of fellow student attending lectures of, as to bill of exchange, 66, 99

BULLEN & LEAKE,
    money counts in, 69

BURDEN OF PROOF,
    of *bona fides* and consideration where there has been fraud, illegality of consideration, duress in respect of bill or note, or improper dealing with it, 142
    what, is cast upon holder where fraud is proved, 143
        must prove not only that he is holder for value, but honest holder for value, 143
    of both honesty and value rests upon plaintiff where fraud, duress, illegality proved, 144

BYLES, J.,
    opinion of, that decisions in *Hartley* v. *Case* and *Solarte* v. *Palmer* had been followed by inconvenience to the public, 164

CAIRNS, LORD,
    judgment of, in *Re The Natal Investment Co.*, 98

CASES,
    importance of selecting best and weightiest, 20

CHANCERY DIVISION,
    common error in, for Judges of, to state too much when dealing only with questions of fact, 4

CHATTELS, PERSONAL,
    not negotiable, except coins of the realm, 51, 55, 57
    paper on which negotiable instruments written, 51, 55

CHEQUE,
    comes into existence by authority of banker, 169
    drawn on banker by his customer, 169
    no acceptance of, 171
    no person can sue banker on, 171
    given for immediate payment and not entitled to days of grace, 171
    may be circulated, 171
        indorsed, 171
    indorser of, may sue drawer, 171

CHEQUE—*continued.*
    indorsee of, may sue indorser, 171
    does not effect assignment of debt due from banker to customer, 171
    is a simple request which banker has promised to comply with, 171
    banker's duty to honour, arises out of promise, express or implied, 173
    banker's refusal to honour, may entitle customer to substantial damages, 173
    customer only can sue banker for refusal to honour, 174
    may be specially indorsed as well as indorsed in blank, 174
        drawn to bearer or order, 174
        post dated, 174
    if indorsement of, forgery, banker who paid formerly not entitled to debit customer with amount, 175
    law altered by 16 & 17 Vict. c. 59, s. 19, 175
    person who has obtained money, when indorsement forged, must return it, 176
    if signature to, forgery, banker not entitled to charge customer, 175
    where amount of, altered, banker can only charge customer amount for which cheque drawn, 176
        unless customer has been negligent and so caused loss, 176
    crossed, course of legislation relating to, 180
    crossing, if any, a material part of, 181
    lawful holder of, may cross, 181, 182
    what constitutes crossing, 182
    specially crossed, what? 182
    customer may waive mistake of banker in paying, 182
    crossed, effect of adding words "not negotiable" to, 183
    negotiability in some respects withdrawn from by statute, 183

CHOSE IN ACTION, OR DEBT,
    not assignable at common law, 74
    assignee of, could sue in assignor's name, giving indemnity, 74
    in equity assignee could sue debtor making assignor a defendant, 75
    procedure to recover debt assigned, when assignor's bankruptcy pleaded, 74
    may be assigned for value by any words which show that one parts with and another becomes owner of debt, 76
    assignee of, must give notice to debtor, 76
    debtor might agree in instrument creating debt that holder should take free from equities between debtor and creditor, 77, 98
    whether such agreement entered into, depends on construction of instrument, 98
    difficulty of deciding whether such agreement entered into, 98
    assignee of, can only in very clear case be sure he is free from equities attaching to, 98

COCKBURN, C.J.,
    observations of in *Goodwin* v. *Robarts* have not affected *Crouch* v. *Crédit Foncier Co.*, 36

COINS OF REALM, CURRENT,
    negotiable, 51, 55, 57
    pass to person who takes them *bonâ fide* for value irrespective of title of person who transfers, 57
    not negotiable because they cannot be identified, 57

COLERIDGE, LORD, C.J.,
    dissented from judgment of majority of Court in *Currie* v. *Misa*, 128

COMMERCE,
    men engaged in, prefer occasional loss to embarrassing transactions by unnecessary inquiries, 6

COMMERCIAL LAW,
    unfortunate that questions relating to, should be determined otherwise than by a Judge and jury, 5

CONSIDERATION,
    given, a criterion of *bona fides*, 22
    important in determining *bona fides*, 22
    adequacy of, sometimes sufficient to establish *bona fides*, 23, 144
    given, sometimes cogent evidence of dishonesty, 23, 26, 144
    need not be full, 26
    illegality of, must be studied as part of general law, 142
    presumption of, for bill of exchange and promissory note, 142
        may be rebutted, 69
    for bill of exchange, does not matter from whom it moves, 67
    stated account not sufficient, for promise to pay *in futuro*, 70

CONSTRUCTIVE NOTICE,
    will not be allowed by House of Lords to enter into domain of negotiability, 17

CONTRACT,
    definition of, "an agreement to which the supreme power has annexed an obligation," 66
    not synonymous with agreement, 67
    is "an agreement plus an obligation," 67
    study of law of, involves same kind of investigation as that pursued by botanist or zoologist in classifying plants or animals, 67
    bill of exchange, a simple, 67

COTTENHAM, LORD,
    judgment of, in *Mangles* v. *Dixon* reversed by Lord St. Leonards, 77

DEBENTURES,
    of English public company not negotiable notwithstanding usage of English market, 36

DIRECTIONS,
    given by Judge to jury in trial at common law as to ownership of bill, 18

DISHONOUR. *See* BILL OF EXCHANGE, PROMISSORY NOTE.
    by non-acceptance, 106
    non-payment, 159
    notice of. *See* BILL OF EXCHANGE, 159

DISGRACED INSTRUMENT, what is, 140
    holder of, cannot have better title to, than person from whom he received it, 140
    transferee of takes subject to equities arising out of original transaction, 140
    what are equities arising out of original transaction, 140

DRAWEE. *See* BILL OF EXCHANGE, 100

DRAWER. *See* BILL OF EXCHANGE, 100 ; CHEQUE, 169

DURESS, what is, 142

ENGLISH INSTRUMENTS,
    cannot be made negotiable by usage or contract, 35, 55
    may be made negotiable by law merchant, 35, 40
    not negotiable, certificates of shares in English companies, 49
        scrip for certificates of shares in do., 49
        probably shares warrants in do., 49

EQUITY,
    Judges, great services rendered by, 17
    has always taken care to guard the beneficial interest, 32
    rule in, that assignee of chose in action takes subject to equities subsisting between assignor and his debtor, 77
    modification of, by Judges, 77

ESTOPPEL,
    title by, differs from negotiability, 14

EVIDENCE,
    not reported in common law reports save so far as necessary to see if direction of Judge correct, or if there was anything to be left to jury, 13

FIGURES,
    in a bill of exchange, are controlled by words denoting the amount, 102
    instrument having, but no words in body, held to be good bill of exchange, 103
    alteration of, held not to constitute material alteration of bill, 103

FOREIGN INSTRUMENTS,
    most important of these relate to public debts of foreign and colonial governments, 41
    steps by which they have been brought within the law relating to negotiable securities, 42 *et seq.*
    when negotiable here, 42, 55
    not necessarily negotiable here, because negotiable abroad, 42, 55
    cannot become negotiable by usage here, if some act, out of England, necessary to pass title to them, 49
    bonds and scrip for bonds of foreign governments, and foreign companies, no duties as to (*e.g.* presentment, notice of dishonour) which exist as to bills of exchange, 58

FORMS,
    bills of exchange, 79—95, 123
        indorsements of, 121
    dividend warrant, 39
    exchequer bill, 37
    promissory notes, 149, 151
    Russian scrip, 44

FRANCE, LAW OF,
    in time of Pothier, required that drawee of bill of exchange should not reside in same town as drawer, 101
    article 111 of Code de Commerce is to the same effect, 101

FRANCE, LAW OF—*continued.*
    does not now require that there shall be three parties to a bill, 104
    otherwise, when Pothier wrote, 104

GENERAL IMPRESSIONS, uselessness of in domain of law, 12

GRACE, DAYS OF.
    See BILL OF EXCHANGE, 71

HERSCHELL, LORD,
    in *Simmons* v. *London Joint Stock Bank*, held that a person who advanced money upon a negotiable instrument acquired a title to the extent of the advance, 31

HOLDER. *See* BILL OF EXCHANGE, BONÂ-FIDE HOLDER, CHEQUE, PROMISSORY NOTE.
    is entitled to recover in action on negotiable instrument although he took it negligently and for inadequate consideration, provided he took it honestly and for value, 145

HOLDER FOR VALUE,
    person who took a promissory note or cheque payable on demand, given in consideration of a past debt, once held not to be a, 126
    such an instrument said to be without consideration because holder could immediately demand payment of his debt, 126

INDORSEMENT. *See* BILL OF EXCHANGE, PROMISSORY NOTE, CHEQUE, blank, special, restrictive

INDORSER. *See* BILL OF EXCHANGE, PROMISSORY NOTE, CHEQUE.

INSTRUMENT,
    if its nature, incidents and effects are defined and regulated by English law cannot be made negotiable by usage, 41
    foreign, may be made negotiable, by usage here, *ib.*

INTEREST,
    not due at common law upon debts apart from agreement, express or implied, 71
    may be due as damages, under 3 & 4 W. 4, c. 42, 71
    due on bill of exchange from maturity, 71

JAMES, L.J.
    judgment of and Mellish, L.J. in *Ex parte Haywood*, that drawing of bill does not relate back to acceptance, 111

JOHNSON, DR.
    line written by in "Deserted Village," 52

KEKEWICH, J.
    in *Simmons* v. *London Joint Stock Bank*, regarded statements of fact by House of Lords in *Sheffield* v. *London Joint Stock Bank*, as equivalent to legal propositions, 5
    observations of, in *Simmons* v. *London Joint Stock Bank* criticised, 19

KNIGHT BRUCE,
    judgment of in *Mangles* v. *Dixon* reversed by Lord Cottenham, C. reinstated by Lord St. Leonards, C., 77

LECTURES,
    reasons for undertaking, 1
    subject of described, 2

LINDLEY, L. J.
    request by, to undertake task of delivering lectures, a command that must be obeyed, 1

LORDS, HOUSE OF,
    service rendered by, to mercantile community in reversing decisions of Court of Appeal in *Sheffield* v. *London Joint Stock Bank* and *Simmons* v. *London Joint Stock Bank*, 4
    no single principle of law established in these decisions, 5
    decisions of in these cases consistent with each other, 28
    grounds of decision of, in *Goodwin* v. *Robarts*, 45
    importance of not confounding the two grounds, 46
    do not seem to have adopted simple principle applied by Lush, J., in *Currie* v. *Misa*, 129

LUSH, J.
    judgment of in *Currie* v. *Misa*, 128
    simple principle applied by, not adopted by House of Lords, 129
    but enacted in s. 27 (*b*) of Bills of Exchange Act, 1882.

MACNAGHTON, LORD,
    expressions used by, in *Sheffield* v. *London Joint Stock Bank*, 15

MANSFIELD, LORD,
    distinctly laid down that question whether an instrument is negotiable, is a question of law to be determined by the Judge, 33
    stated that he was wrong in allowing evidence of usage to be given to show that an instrument was not negotiable, when it had been judicially held to be negotiable, 33

MARTIN, BARON,
    dictum of, that Judge should state finding of fact, or inference of fact without giving reasons, 4
    practical skill of, in trying action on a bill of exchange where question of fraud involved, 23

MELLISH, L.J.
    judgment of and of James, L. J., that drawing of bill does not relate back to acceptance, 111

MISCHIEF,
    arising from Judges stating too much when dealing with questions of fact, 4
    illustrated by cases of *Sheffield* v. *London Joint Stock Bank* and *Simmons* v. *London Joint Stock Bank*, 4

NEGOTIABILITY,
    principal element in, the acquisition of an instrument by a person who takes *bonâ fide* and for value, though the true owner has not been a party to the transaction by which the property has been taken, 10
    the acquisition of property by your own act, not another's, 10
    transferability by delivery not, 10
        difference illustrated, 10
    cannot be inferred from transferability by delivery, 10
    instance of forgetfulness of true meaning of, 12
    so called, by conduct, by estoppel, 14
    has nothing to do with conduct of owner, 14
        or with estoppel, 14

NEGOTIABILITY—*continued.*
    differs from title by estoppel, 14
    doctrine of, speaks for honesty of commercial men, 16
    property with incidents of, created in this country by merchants of City of London, 17
    element of, cannot be added to instrument created here by any usage, 33
    private persons cannot attach incident of, to property by contract or usage, 35
    stipulation between obligor and obligee that obligor may pay any holder, falls short of negotiability, 36
    though such stipulation perfectly good, and payment under it good as against obligee, 36
    may be added by statute, 35, 40
    steps by which incident of, applied to foreign instruments, 42
    judges could not have given effect to usage in case of English instruments, 43
    by usage, first applied to bonds of foreign governments, 46
        as to these no contract subsists, no right of action, 47
    then to scrip for bonds of foreign governments, 46
    then to bonds of foreign companies, 46
    if negotiable by usage of English market, 46
    by usage of foreign instruments, usage applies only to acquisition of property in paper and not to enforcement of engagement 47
    "elements of," objection to phrase, 51
    "elements of," phrase inapplicable to personal chattels, 51
    true view of, that a man can claim property in negotiable instruments by what he has done, not by what anybody else has done, 57

NEGOTIABLE,
    importance of knowing determinate ideas involved in word, 4
    perils arising from forgetfulness of meaning of, illustrated, 4
    instrument, what is, 6
    Court will decide whether instrument is, 7
    except where negotiability rests upon usage, 7
    instrument not, if such, and in such a state that some act other than delivery required to pass the contract, 7
    in considering whether instrument is, importance of keeping in mind its nature and condition, 7
    bill of exchange, when not, 8
    instrument to be, must be in such a state that the true owner could pass the property in it by delivery, 9
    instrument, definition of, not satisfied by saying it is one the property in which passes by delivery from hand to hand, 9
    by delivery, tendency to mislead of phrase in Bills of Exchange Act, 1882, 11
    instrument not, unless the true owner could pass the property in it by delivery, and unless everybody who takes *bonâ fide* and for value, acquires a good title, 13
    instrument, *bonâ-fide* holder of, claims not by virtue of any estate or interest created by the true owner, but by virtue of having taken the instrument honestly and for value, 16
    instrument, person taking not bound to make inquiries, 17
                    but bound to be honest, 17
                    is not honest if he refrains from making inquiries because he suspects there is something wrong, 17

NEGOTIABLE —*continued*.
  instrument, person taking with knowledge that transferor has only limited interest cannot acquire more than that limited interest, 17, 28
  securities, transactions in regard to must be passed through quickly, 18
  instrument, person advancing money upon, obtains a good security to extent of his advance, 31
  whether instrument is, or not, question for Judge, 33
    who must not, where English instrument is concerned, hear evidence on the point, 33
  instrument, document containing promises other than promise to pay money cannot be a, 35
  English instruments not, by usage or stipulation, 35, 55
    but only by the Law Merchant, or Statute, 35, 40
  foreign instruments may be, by English Courts adopting usage of our markets, 41
    but not if instrument shows on its face that it will not pass by mere delivery, 42
  instruments, abroad, not necessarily negotiable here, 42
  securities, steps by which foreign instruments have been brought within the law relating to, 42
  personal chattels, not, 51, 55
    except coins of the realm, 51, 55, 57
      paper on which negotiable instrument is written, 51, 55
  bill of lading, not, 56

NEGOTIABLE SECURITIES,
  list of, 53
    English Instruments—
      bills of exchange ⎫ if in such a state that the true owner
      cheque   ⎬ could pass the property in them by mere
      promissory notes ⎭ delivery, 37
      Bank of England notes, 37
      dividend warrants, if payable to named person or order; now perhaps without words "or order," sec. 8 (4) Bills of Exchange Act, 1882, 40
        form of, 39
      East India bonds, perhaps : see *Taylor* v. *Kymer*, 3 B. & Al. 40
      Exchequer bills, form of, 37
        if blank not filled up, 37
        if blank filled up, and instrument indorsed by person whose name is inserted, 38
    Foreign Instruments—
      Baltimore & Potomac Railway bonds, 48
        unless name inserted, 48
        if name inserted, they can only be transferred by entry in books of the company, 48
      Cedulas, bonds of Buenos Ayres Land Mortgage Bank, 53
      Delaware & Hudson Railway bonds, 48
      Egyptian Government Preference, 47
      Egyptian Unified, 47
      New South Wales, 47
      New York, Pennsylvania & Ohio Railway bonds, 48
      Prussian bonds, 43
      Russian scrip, 44
        form of, 44

PARKE, B.,
    dictum of, in *Peto* v. *Reynolds*, 101
    statement by, as to what is sufficient notice of dishonour, 165

PEARSON, J.,
    decision of, in *Easton* v. *London Joint Stock Bank*, 5

PENNSYLVANIAN RAILROAD,
    certificate of shares not negotiable, 7

PERILS,
    to which law of negotiable securities lately exposed, 4

PERSONAL CHATTELS,
    not negotiable, 55
        except coins of the realm, 51, 55, 57
            paper on which negotiable instrument written, 51, 55
    better title to, cannot be acquired than that of transferor, 55
        except as regards goods bought in market overt, 56
            goods bought from one who obtained them under a contract induced by fraud, but unrescinded, 56
            goods mentioned in a bill of lading which is transferred to a person who takes *bonâ fide* and for value, 56

POTHIER,
    according to, bill of exchange cannot be drawn upon resident of same town as drawer, 101
        bill of exchange must have three parties, drawer, drawee, payee, 104

PRIVATE PERSONS,
    cannot contract to attach to property liability to have owner's title divested, if thief or finder can find *bonâ fide* purchaser, 35
    such incident can be attached only by Law Merchant, or statute, 35

PROMISSORY NOTE,
    instrument under seal not a, 35
    ordinary form of, 149
    maker of in position of acceptor of bill of exchange, 167
    no need to present for payment to maker, 167
    unless promise to pay qualified by place, 167
    first indorser of, if not payable to maker's order, in position of drawer of bill of exchange, 167
        has practically same responsibilities and privileges as indorser of bill of exchange, 167
    instrument payable to maker's own order not a promissory note till indorsed by maker, 167
        form of such note, 151
    may be made payable to bearer, 167
    Bank of England note, instance of, 167
    instrument to be a perfect, must be delivered, 167
    irregular instruments, 168

PROMISSORY NOTE—*continued.*
  may be indorsed and dealt with as if it were a bill of exchange, 168
  dishonour of,
    notice of, must be given to first indorser if he is not maker, 168
    to charge indorser of, presentment necessary, 168
  payable on demand, must be presented within reasonable time after indorsement, 168
    or indorser will be discharged, 168
  not presented within reasonable time, holder for value affected only by defects of which he had notice, and not by all equities arising out of note, 168
  payable on demand, when disgraced, 140

RAPHAEL v. *TUCK*,
  what case settled, 21
  destroyed doctrine that a man who took a bill of exchange carelessly and not in such a way as a prudent man would have taken it could not recover, although he took it honestly and for value, 22
  observations of Jervis, C.J., on affidavit by juryman in, 21

REASONS
  for undertaking task of delivering lectures, 1

ROLLS, MASTER OF,
  cases admirably reported by present, in old Queen's Bench Reports, 39

ROLT, L.J.,
  decision of, in *Re Blakely Ordnance Co.*, 98

ST. LEONARDS, LORD,
  magnificent judgment of, in *Mangles* v. *Dixon*, 77
  satirical references of, to common law lawyers, labouring to apply a half apprehended equity, 77

STATUTES,
  51 Geo. 3, c. 64...40
  1 & 2 Geo. 4, c. 78...107, 108
  3 & 4 W. 4, c. 42...71
  16 & 17 Vict. c. 59...175
  19 & 20 Vict. c. 25...180, 181
              97...107
  21 & 22 Vict. c. 79...180, 181
  30 & 31 Vict. c. 131...49, 50, 51
  39 & 40 Vict. c. 81...181, 182, 185
  41 Vict. c. 13...109
  45 & 46 Vict. c. 61...11, 40, 65, 97, 105, 115, 129, 130, 138, 153, 158, 180, 183

TIME,
  reasonable, difficulty of determining, 154
    regard must be had to all the circumstances, 154
    no fixed rule for determining, 154
  See BILL OF EXCHANGE,
    presentment for acceptance, presentment for payment, notice of dishonour.

TORTS,
  importance of not placing under law relating to, obligations arising out of contract, 172

WILLES, J.,
  discussion by, in *Fuentes* v. *Montis*, of question under what circumstances a man can acquire a better title to chattels than the man has with whom he deals, 56

THE END.

www.ingramcontent.com/pod-product-compliance
Lightning Source LLC
Chambersburg PA
CBHW031816220426
43662CB00007B/666